Ancient Shushan HaBira above the City

Persian King Worshiping Ahura Mazda

The Anatomy of the Book of Esther

Published 2012
Includes traditional Hebrew text and royal English translation
ISBN 978-0-9667019-2-0
Copyright © 2011
Second Printing, 2012
by Rick Arons

Published by
BS"D Press

For information on this and other publications, contact BS"D Press.
www.BSDPress.com

The Anatomy of the Book of Esther

Contents

Is the Book of Esther Fact or Fiction?

.... **Page 4**

Blessings before the Reading

....**Page 6**

Complete Hebrew Text

.... **Page 7**

Blessing after the Reading

.... **Page 29**

Shoshanat Yaacov

.... **Page 30**

English Translation and
Original Commentary

.... **Page 32**

Fact or Fiction?

Is the Book of Esther fact or fiction? Is religious tradition the only evidence that testifies to its veracity?

Lewis B. Paton wrote in his 1908 commentary, *"It is doubtful whether even a historical kernel underlies its narrative."*

More recently Jon D. Levenson (in his 1997 commentary) called the book "comical" and "a farce." *"The historical problems with Esther are so massive as to persuade anyone who is not already obligated by religious dogma to believe in the historicity of the biblical narrative to doubt the veracity of the narrative."*

Adele Berlin, writing for the 2003 **JPS Bible Commentary** series holds a similar opinion. *"The story itself is implausible as history and, as many scholars now agree, it is better viewed as imaginative storytelling, not unlike others that circulated in the Persian and Hellenistic periods among Jews of the Land of Israel and of the Diaspora."*

Carey A. Moore, the author of the **Anchor Bible** commentary on Esther asserts that many elements of the Esther story are just not believable and that the account is not different from many other historically fictitious stories.

Many, then, see the Megillah as a contrived folk-tale – little more than an engaging fiction serving as the rationale for an enduring, light-hearted celebration. But, if religious faith and practice can be based on a complete fiction, then what does that say about the underlying value of that faith? If one credits faith for survival, then the events that led to the perpetuation and institutionalization of that faith ought to be largely verifiable -- at the very least, circumstantially.

The commentary that follows speaks directly to this issue.

An historical scenario is assembled within which the events of the Megillah fit comfortably. The behavior of the principals is rational and their motivations clear. The history is supported by archaeological finds as well as by citations in contemporaneous or later literary and religious works.

In sum, while the author may have shaped the story to enhance its impact, the argument for historical accuracy is strong. And with this evidentiary support, our story assumes its rightful place in the ancient faith narrative.

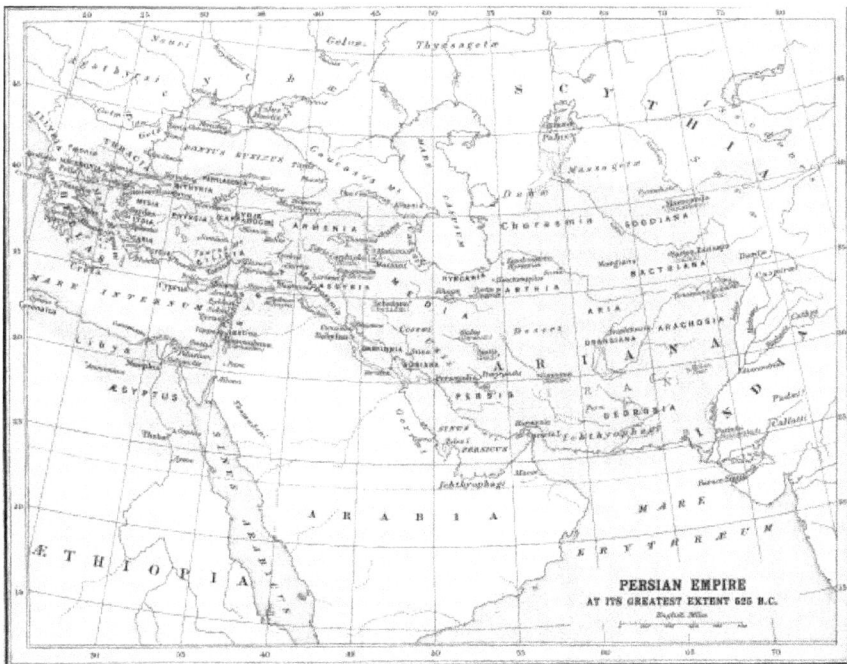

PERSIAN EMPIRE
AT ITS GREATEST EXTENT 525 B.C.

Preliminary Blessings

The reading of the *Book of Esther* is preceded by three blessings.

The first reflects the status of this reading as the fulfillment of a religious obligation. The second testifies to the miraculous nature of the event as retold in the *Book of Esther*. The third acknowledges our gratitude for being present to celebrate this occasion once again this year, just as the Jewish people have done for more than two millennia.

בָּרוּךְ אַתָּה יְיָ, אֱלֹהֵינוּ מֶלֶךְ הָעוֹלָם, אֲשֶׁר קִדְּשָׁנוּ בְּמִצְוֹתָיו, וְצִוָּנוּ: עַל מִקְרָא מְגִלָּה.

Blessed are You, Lord our God, King of the universe, who has sanctified us with His commandments, and commanded us concerning the reading of the Megillah. (Cong.— *Amen.*)

בָּרוּךְ אַתָּה יְיָ, אֱלֹהֵינוּ מֶלֶךְ הָעוֹלָם, שֶׁעָשָׂה נִסִּים לַאֲבוֹתֵינוּ, בַּיָּמִים הָהֵם בִּזְמַן הַזֶּה:

Blessed are You, Lord our God, King of the universe, who performed miracles for our forefathers in those days, at this time. (Cong.— *Amen.*)

(During the morning reading of the Megillah, remember that the following blessing pertains to the other Purim mitzvot as well: the sending of food portions, gifts to the poor and the Purim feast.)

בָּרוּךְ אַתָּה יְיָ, אֱלֹהֵינוּ מֶלֶךְ הָעוֹלָם, שֶׁהֶחֱיָנוּ וְקִיְּמָנוּ וְהִגִּיעָנוּ לִזְמַן הַזֶּה.

Blessed are You, Lord our God, King of the universe, who has granted us life, sustained us, and enabled us to reach this occasion. (Cong.— *Amen.*)

Esther Chapter 1

א וַיְהִי, בִּימֵי אֲחַשְׁוֵרוֹשׁ: הוּא אֲחַשְׁוֵרוֹשׁ, הַמֹּלֵךְ מֵהֹדּוּ וְעַד-כּוּשׁ--שֶׁבַע וְעֶשְׂרִים וּמֵאָה, מְדִינָה.

ב בַּיָּמִים, הָהֵם--כְּשֶׁבֶת הַמֶּלֶךְ אֲחַשְׁוֵרוֹשׁ, עַל כִּסֵּא מַלְכוּתוֹ, אֲשֶׁר, בְּשׁוּשַׁן הַבִּירָה.

ג בִּשְׁנַת שָׁלוֹשׁ, לְמָלְכוֹ, עָשָׂה מִשְׁתֶּה, לְכָל-שָׂרָיו וַעֲבָדָיו: חֵיל פָּרַס וּמָדַי, הַפַּרְתְּמִים וְשָׂרֵי הַמְּדִינוֹת-- לְפָנָיו.

ד בְּהַרְאֹתוֹ, אֶת-עֹשֶׁר כְּבוֹד מַלְכוּתוֹ, וְאֶת-יְקָר, תִּפְאֶרֶת גְּדוּלָתוֹ; יָמִים רַבִּים, שְׁמוֹנִים וּמְאַת יוֹם.

ה וּבִמְלוֹאת הַיָּמִים הָאֵלֶּה, עָשָׂה הַמֶּלֶךְ לְכָל-הָעָם הַנִּמְצְאִים בְּשׁוּשַׁן הַבִּירָה לְמִגָּדוֹל וְעַד-קָטָן מִשְׁתֶּה-- שִׁבְעַת יָמִים: בַּחֲצַר, גִּנַּת בִּיתַן הַמֶּלֶךְ.

ו חוּר כַּרְפַּס וּתְכֵלֶת, אָחוּז בְּחַבְלֵי-בוּץ וְאַרְגָּמָן, עַל-גְּלִילֵי כֶסֶף, וְעַמּוּדֵי שֵׁשׁ; מִטּוֹת זָהָב וָכֶסֶף, עַל רִצְפַת בַּהַט-וָשֵׁשׁ--וְדַר וְסֹחָרֶת.

ז וְהַשְׁקוֹת בִּכְלֵי זָהָב, וְכֵלִים מִכֵּלִים שׁוֹנִים; וְיֵין מַלְכוּת רָב, כְּיַד הַמֶּלֶךְ.

ח וְהַשְּׁתִיָּה כַדָּת, אֵין אֹנֵס: כִּי-כֵן יִסַּד הַמֶּלֶךְ, עַל כָּל-רַב בֵּיתוֹ--לַעֲשׂוֹת, כִּרְצוֹן אִישׁ-וָאִישׁ.

ט גַּם וַשְׁתִּי הַמַּלְכָּה, עָשְׂתָה מִשְׁתֵּה נָשִׁים--בֵּית, הַמַּלְכוּת, אֲשֶׁר, לַמֶּלֶךְ אֲחַשְׁוֵרוֹשׁ.

י בַּיּוֹם, הַשְּׁבִיעִי, כְּטוֹב לֵב-הַמֶּלֶךְ, בַּיָּיִן--אָמַר לִמְהוּמָן בִּזְּתָא חַרְבוֹנָא בִּגְתָא וַאֲבַגְתָא, זֵתַר וְכַרְכַּס, שִׁבְעַת הַסָּרִיסִים, הַמְשָׁרְתִים אֶת-פְּנֵי הַמֶּלֶךְ אֲחַשְׁוֵרוֹשׁ

יא לְהָבִיא אֶת-וַשְׁתִּי הַמַּלְכָּה, לִפְנֵי הַמֶּלֶךְ--בְּכֶתֶר מַלְכוּת: לְהַרְאוֹת הָעַמִּים וְהַשָּׂרִים אֶת-יָפְיָהּ, כִּי-טוֹבַת מַרְאֶה הִיא.

יב וַתְּמָאֵן הַמַּלְכָּה וַשְׁתִּי, לָבוֹא בִּדְבַר הַמֶּלֶךְ, אֲשֶׁר, בְּיַד הַסָּרִיסִים; וַיִּקְצֹף הַמֶּלֶךְ מְאֹד, וַחֲמָתוֹ בָּעֲרָה בוֹ.

יג וַיֹּאמֶר הַמֶּלֶךְ, לַחֲכָמִים יֹדְעֵי הָעִתִּים: כִּי-כֵן, דְּבַר הַמֶּלֶךְ, לִפְנֵי, כָּל-יֹדְעֵי דָּת וָדִין.

יד וְהַקָּרֹב אֵלָיו, כַּרְשְׁנָא שֵׁתָר אַדְמָתָא תַרְשִׁישׁ, מֶרֶס מַרְסְנָא, מְמוּכָן--שִׁבְעַת שָׂרֵי פָּרַס וּמָדַי, רֹאֵי פְּנֵי הַמֶּלֶךְ, הַיֹּשְׁבִים רִאשֹׁנָה, בַּמַּלְכוּת.

טו כְּדָת, מַה-לַּעֲשׂוֹת, בַּמַּלְכָּה, וַשְׁתִּי--עַל אֲשֶׁר לֹא-עָשְׂתָה, אֶת-מַאֲמַר הַמֶּלֶךְ אֲחַשְׁוֵרוֹשׁ, בְּיַד, הַסָּרִיסִים.

טז וַיֹּאמֶר מוֹמְכָן (מְמוּכָן), לִפְנֵי הַמֶּלֶךְ וְהַשָּׂרִים, לֹא עַל-הַמֶּלֶךְ לְבַדּוֹ, עָוְתָה וַשְׁתִּי הַמַּלְכָּה: כִּי עַל-כָּל-הַשָּׂרִים, וְעַל-כָּל-הָעַמִּים, אֲשֶׁר, בְּכָל-מְדִינוֹת הַמֶּלֶךְ אֲחַשְׁוֵרוֹשׁ.

יז כִּי-יֵצֵא דְבַר-הַמַּלְכָּה עַל-כָּל-הַנָּשִׁים, לְהַבְזוֹת בַּעְלֵיהֶן בְּעֵינֵיהֶן: בְּאָמְרָם, הַמֶּלֶךְ אֲחַשְׁוֵרוֹשׁ אָמַר לְהָבִיא אֶת-וַשְׁתִּי הַמַּלְכָּה לְפָנָיו--וְלֹא-בָאָה.

יח וְהַיּוֹם הַזֶּה תֹּאמַרְנָה שָׂרוֹת פָּרַס-וּמָדַי, אֲשֶׁר שָׁמְעוּ אֶת-דְּבַר הַמַּלְכָּה, לְכֹל, שָׂרֵי הַמֶּלֶךְ; וּכְדַי, בִּזָּיוֹן וָקָצֶף.

יט אִם-עַל-הַמֶּלֶךְ טוֹב, יֵצֵא דְבַר-מַלְכוּת מִלְּפָנָיו, וְיִכָּתֵב בְּדָתֵי פָרַס-וּמָדַי, וְלֹא יַעֲבוֹר: אֲשֶׁר לֹא-תָבוֹא וַשְׁתִּי, לִפְנֵי הַמֶּלֶךְ אֲחַשְׁוֵרוֹשׁ, וּמַלְכוּתָהּ יִתֵּן הַמֶּלֶךְ, לִרְעוּתָהּ הַטּוֹבָה מִמֶּנָּה.

כ וְנִשְׁמַע פִּתְגָם הַמֶּלֶךְ אֲשֶׁר-יַעֲשֶׂה בְּכָל-מַלְכוּתוֹ, כִּי רַבָּה הִיא; וְכָל-הַנָּשִׁים, יִתְּנוּ יְקָר לְבַעְלֵיהֶן--לְמִגָּדוֹל, וְעַד-קָטָן.

כא וַיִּיטַב, הַדָּבָר, בְּעֵינֵי הַמֶּלֶךְ, וְהַשָּׂרִים; וַיַּעַשׂ הַמֶּלֶךְ, כִּדְבַר מְמוּכָן.

כב וַיִּשְׁלַח סְפָרִים, אֶל-כָּל-מְדִינוֹת הַמֶּלֶךְ--אֶל-מְדִינָה וּמְדִינָה כִּכְתָבָהּ, וְאֶל-עַם וָעָם כִּלְשׁוֹנוֹ: לִהְיוֹת כָּל-אִישׁ שֹׂרֵר בְּבֵיתוֹ, וּמְדַבֵּר כִּלְשׁוֹן עַמּוֹ.

Esther Chapter 2

א אַחַר הַדְּבָרִים הָאֵלֶּה, כְּשֹׁךְ, חֲמַת הַמֶּלֶךְ אֲחַשְׁוֵרוֹשׁ-זָכַר אֶת-וַשְׁתִּי וְאֵת אֲשֶׁר-עָשָׂתָה, וְאֵת אֲשֶׁר-נִגְזַר עָלֶיהָ.

ב וַיֹּאמְרוּ נַעֲרֵי-הַמֶּלֶךְ, מְשָׁרְתָיו: יְבַקְשׁוּ לַמֶּלֶךְ נְעָרוֹת בְּתוּלוֹת, טוֹבוֹת מַרְאֶה.

ג וְיַפְקֵד הַמֶּלֶךְ פְּקִידִים, בְּכָל-מְדִינוֹת מַלְכוּתוֹ, וְיִקְבְּצוּ אֶת-כָּל-נַעֲרָה-בְתוּלָה טוֹבַת מַרְאֶה אֶל-שׁוּשַׁן הַבִּירָה

אֶל-בֵּית הַנָּשִׁים, אֶל-יַד הֵגֶא סְרִיס הַמֶּלֶךְ שֹׁמֵר הַנָּשִׁים; וְנָתוֹן, תַּמְרֻקֵיהֶן.

ד וְהַנַּעֲרָה, אֲשֶׁר תִּיטַב בְּעֵינֵי הַמֶּלֶךְ--תִּמְלֹךְ, תַּחַת וַשְׁתִּי; וַיִּיטַב הַדָּבָר בְּעֵינֵי הַמֶּלֶךְ, וַיַּעַשׂ כֵּן.

ה אִישׁ יְהוּדִי, הָיָה בְּשׁוּשַׁן הַבִּירָה; וּשְׁמוֹ מָרְדֳּכַי, בֶּן יָאִיר בֶּן-שִׁמְעִי בֶּן-קִישׁ--אִישׁ יְמִינִי.

ו אֲשֶׁר הָגְלָה, מִירוּשָׁלַיִם, עִם-הַגֹּלָה אֲשֶׁר הָגְלְתָה, עִם יְכָנְיָה מֶלֶךְ-יְהוּדָה--אֲשֶׁר הֶגְלָה, נְבוּכַדְנֶצַּר מֶלֶךְ בָּבֶל.

ז וַיְהִי אֹמֵן אֶת-הֲדַסָּה, הִיא אֶסְתֵּר בַּת-דֹּדוֹ--כִּי אֵין לָהּ, אָב וָאֵם; וְהַנַּעֲרָה יְפַת-תֹּאַר, וְטוֹבַת מַרְאֶה, וּבְמוֹת אָבִיהָ וְאִמָּהּ, לְקָחָהּ מָרְדֳּכַי לוֹ לְבַת.

ח וַיְהִי, בְּהִשָּׁמַע דְּבַר-הַמֶּלֶךְ וְדָתוֹ, וּבְהִקָּבֵץ נְעָרוֹת רַבּוֹת אֶל-שׁוּשַׁן הַבִּירָה, אֶל-יַד הֵגָי; וַתִּלָּקַח אֶסְתֵּר אֶל-בֵּית הַמֶּלֶךְ, אֶל-יַד הֵגַי שֹׁמֵר הַנָּשִׁים.

ט וַתִּיטַב הַנַּעֲרָה בְעֵינָיו, וַתִּשָּׂא חֶסֶד לְפָנָיו, וַיְבַהֵל אֶת-תַּמְרוּקֶיהָ וְאֶת-מָנוֹתֶהָ לָתֵת לָהּ, וְאֵת שֶׁבַע הַנְּעָרוֹת הָרְאֻיוֹת לָתֶת-לָהּ מִבֵּית הַמֶּלֶךְ; וַיְשַׁנֶּהָ וְאֶת-נַעֲרוֹתֶיהָ לְטוֹב, בֵּית הַנָּשִׁים.

י לֹא-הִגִּידָה אֶסְתֵּר, אֶת-עַמָּהּ וְאֶת-מוֹלַדְתָּהּ: כִּי מָרְדֳּכַי צִוָּה עָלֶיהָ, אֲשֶׁר לֹא-תַגִּיד.

יא וּבְכָל-יוֹם וָיוֹם--מָרְדֳּכַי מִתְהַלֵּךְ, לִפְנֵי חֲצַר בֵּית-הַנָּשִׁים: לָדַעַת אֶת-שְׁלוֹם אֶסְתֵּר, וּמַה-יֵּעָשֶׂה בָּהּ.

יב וּבְהַגִּיעַ תֹּר נַעֲרָה וְנַעֲרָה לָבוֹא אֶל-הַמֶּלֶךְ אֲחַשְׁוֵרוֹשׁ, מִקֵּץ הֱיוֹת לָהּ כְּדָת הַנָּשִׁים שְׁנֵים עָשָׂר חֹדֶשׁ--כִּי כֵּן יִמְלְאוּ, יְמֵי מְרוּקֵיהֶן: שִׁשָּׁה חֳדָשִׁים, בְּשֶׁמֶן הַמֹּר, וְשִׁשָּׁה חֳדָשִׁים בַּבְּשָׂמִים, וּבְתַמְרוּקֵי הַנָּשִׁים.

יג וּבָזֶה, הַנַּעֲרָה בָּאָה אֶל-הַמֶּלֶךְ אֵת כָּל-אֲשֶׁר תֹּאמַר יִנָּתֵן לָהּ, לָבוֹא עִמָּהּ, מִבֵּית הַנָּשִׁים, עַד-בֵּית הַמֶּלֶךְ.

יד בָּעֶרֶב הִיא בָאָה, וּבַבֹּקֶר הִיא שָׁבָה אֶל-בֵּית הַנָּשִׁים שֵׁנִי, אֶל-יַד שַׁעַשְׁגַז סְרִיס הַמֶּלֶךְ, שֹׁמֵר הַפִּילַגְשִׁים: לֹא-תָבוֹא עוֹד אֶל-הַמֶּלֶךְ, כִּי אִם-חָפֵץ בָּהּ הַמֶּלֶךְ וְנִקְרְאָה בְשֵׁם.

טו וּבְהַגִּיעַ תֹּר-אֶסְתֵּר בַּת-אֲבִיחַיִל דֹּד מָרְדֳּכַי אֲשֶׁר לָקַח-לוֹ לְבַת לָבוֹא אֶל-הַמֶּלֶךְ, לֹא בִקְשָׁה דָּבָר--כִּי אִם אֶת-אֲשֶׁר יֹאמַר הֵגַי סְרִיס-הַמֶּלֶךְ, שֹׁמֵר הַנָּשִׁים; וַתְּהִי אֶסְתֵּר נֹשֵׂאת חֵן, בְּעֵינֵי כָּל-רֹאֶיהָ.

טז וַתִּלָּקַח אֶסְתֵּר אֶל-הַמֶּלֶךְ אֲחַשְׁוֵרוֹשׁ, אֶל-בֵּית מַלְכוּתוֹ, בַּחֹדֶשׁ הָעֲשִׂירִי, הוּא-חֹדֶשׁ טֵבֵת--בִּשְׁנַת-שֶׁבַע, לְמַלְכוּתוֹ.

יז וַיֶּאֱהַב הַמֶּלֶךְ אֶת-אֶסְתֵּר מִכָּל-הַנָּשִׁים, וַתִּשָּׂא-חֵן וָחֶסֶד לְפָנָיו מִכָּל-הַבְּתוּלוֹת; וַיָּשֶׂם כֶּתֶר-מַלְכוּת בְּרֹאשָׁהּ, וַיַּמְלִיכֶהָ תַּחַת וַשְׁתִּי.

יח וַיַּעַשׂ הַמֶּלֶךְ מִשְׁתֶּה גָדוֹל, לְכָל-שָׂרָיו וַעֲבָדָיו--אֵת, מִשְׁתֵּה אֶסְתֵּר; וַהֲנָחָה לַמְּדִינוֹת עָשָׂה, וַיִּתֵּן מַשְׂאֵת כְּיַד הַמֶּלֶךְ.

יט וּבְהִקָּבֵץ בְּתוּלוֹת, שֵׁנִית; וּמָרְדֳּכַי, יֹשֵׁב בְּשַׁעַר-הַמֶּלֶךְ.

כ אֵין אֶסְתֵּר, מַגֶּדֶת מוֹלַדְתָּהּ וְאֶת-עַמָּהּ, כַּאֲשֶׁר צִוָּה עָלֶיהָ, מָרְדֳּכָי; וְאֶת-מַאֲמַר מָרְדֳּכַי אֶסְתֵּר עֹשָׂה, כַּאֲשֶׁר הָיְתָה בְאָמְנָה אִתּוֹ.

כא בַּיָּמִים הָהֵם, וּמָרְדֳּכַי יוֹשֵׁב בְּשַׁעַר-הַמֶּלֶךְ; קָצַף בִּגְתָן וָתֶרֶשׁ שְׁנֵי-סָרִיסֵי הַמֶּלֶךְ, מִשֹּׁמְרֵי הַסַּף, וַיְבַקְשׁוּ לִשְׁלֹחַ יָד, בַּמֶּלֶךְ אֲחַשְׁוֵרֹשׁ.

כב וַיִּוָּדַע הַדָּבָר לְמָרְדֳּכַי, וַיַּגֵּד לְאֶסְתֵּר הַמַּלְכָּה; וַתֹּאמֶר אֶסְתֵּר לַמֶּלֶךְ, בְּשֵׁם מָרְדֳּכָי.

כג וַיְבֻקַּשׁ הַדָּבָר וַיִּמָּצֵא, וַיִּתָּלוּ שְׁנֵיהֶם עַל-עֵץ; וַיִּכָּתֵב, בְּסֵפֶר דִּבְרֵי הַיָּמִים--לִפְנֵי הַמֶּלֶךְ.

Esther Chapter 3

א אַחַר הַדְּבָרִים הָאֵלֶּה, גִּדַּל הַמֶּלֶךְ אֲחַשְׁוֵרוֹשׁ אֶת-הָמָן בֶּן-הַמְּדָתָא הָאֲגָגִי--וַיְנַשְּׂאֵהוּ וַיָּשֶׂם אֶת-כִּסְאוֹ, מֵעַל, כָּל-הַשָּׂרִים אֲשֶׁר אִתּוֹ.

ב וְכָל-עַבְדֵי הַמֶּלֶךְ אֲשֶׁר-בְּשַׁעַר הַמֶּלֶךְ, כֹּרְעִים וּמִשְׁתַּחֲוִים לְהָמָן--כִּי-כֵן, צִוָּה-לוֹ הַמֶּלֶךְ; וּמָרְדֳּכַי--לֹא יִכְרַע, וְלֹא יִשְׁתַּחֲוֶה.

ג וַיֹּאמְרוּ עַבְדֵי הַמֶּלֶךְ, אֲשֶׁר-בְּשַׁעַר הַמֶּלֶךְ--
לְמָרְדֳּכָי: מַדּוּעַ אַתָּה עוֹבֵר, אֵת מִצְוַת הַמֶּלֶךְ.

ד וַיְהִי, באמרם (כְּאָמְרָם) אֵלָיו יוֹם וָיוֹם, וְלֹא שָׁמַע
אֲלֵיהֶם; וַיַּגִּידוּ לְהָמָן, לִרְאוֹת הֲיַעַמְדוּ דִּבְרֵי מָרְדֳּכַי--
כִּי-הִגִּיד לָהֶם, אֲשֶׁר-הוּא יְהוּדִי.

ה וַיַּרְא הָמָן--כִּי-אֵין מָרְדֳּכַי, כֹּרֵעַ וּמִשְׁתַּחֲוֶה לוֹ;
וַיִּמָּלֵא הָמָן חֵמָה.

ו וַיִּבֶז בְּעֵינָיו, לִשְׁלֹחַ יָד בְּמָרְדֳּכַי לְבַדּוֹ--כִּי-הִגִּידוּ לוֹ,
אֶת-עַם מָרְדֳּכָי; וַיְבַקֵּשׁ הָמָן, לְהַשְׁמִיד אֶת-כָּל-הַיְּהוּדִים
אֲשֶׁר בְּכָל-מַלְכוּת אֲחַשְׁוֵרוֹשׁ--עַם מָרְדֳּכָי.

ז בַּחֹדֶשׁ הָרִאשׁוֹן, הוּא-חֹדֶשׁ נִיסָן, בִּשְׁנַת שְׁתֵּים
עֶשְׂרֵה, לַמֶּלֶךְ אֲחַשְׁוֵרוֹשׁ: הִפִּיל פּוּר הוּא הַגּוֹרָל לִפְנֵי
הָמָן, מִיּוֹם לְיוֹם וּמֵחֹדֶשׁ לְחֹדֶשׁ שְׁנֵים-עָשָׂר--הוּא-
חֹדֶשׁ אֲדָר.

ח וַיֹּאמֶר הָמָן, לַמֶּלֶךְ אֲחַשְׁוֵרוֹשׁ--יֶשְׁנוֹ עַם-אֶחָד מְפֻזָּר
וּמְפֹרָד בֵּין הָעַמִּים, בְּכֹל מְדִינוֹת מַלְכוּתֶךָ; וְדָתֵיהֶם
שֹׁנוֹת מִכָּל-עָם, וְאֶת-דָּתֵי הַמֶּלֶךְ אֵינָם עֹשִׂים, וְלַמֶּלֶךְ
אֵין-שֹׁוֶה, לְהַנִּיחָם.

ט אִם-עַל-הַמֶּלֶךְ טוֹב, יִכָּתֵב לְאַבְּדָם; וַעֲשֶׂרֶת אֲלָפִים
כִּכַּר-כֶּסֶף, אֶשְׁקוֹל עַל-יְדֵי עֹשֵׂי הַמְּלָאכָה, לְהָבִיא, אֶל-
גִּנְזֵי הַמֶּלֶךְ.

י וַיָּסַר הַמֶּלֶךְ אֶת-טַבַּעְתּוֹ, מֵעַל יָדוֹ; וַיִּתְּנָהּ, לְהָמָן בֶּן-
הַמְּדָתָא הָאֲגָגִי--צֹרֵר הַיְּהוּדִים.

יא וַיֹּאמֶר הַמֶּלֶךְ לְהָמָן, הַכֶּסֶף נָתוּן לָךְ; וְהָעָם, לַעֲשׂוֹת בּוֹ כַּטּוֹב בְּעֵינֶיךָ.

יב וַיִּקָּרְאוּ סֹפְרֵי הַמֶּלֶךְ בַּחֹדֶשׁ הָרִאשׁוֹן, בִּשְׁלוֹשָׁה עָשָׂר יוֹם בּוֹ, וַיִּכָּתֵב כְּכָל-אֲשֶׁר-צִוָּה הָמָן אֶל אֲחַשְׁדַּרְפְּנֵי-הַמֶּלֶךְ וְאֶל-הַפַּחוֹת אֲשֶׁר עַל-מְדִינָה וּמְדִינָה וְאֶל-שָׂרֵי עַם וָעָם, מְדִינָה וּמְדִינָה כִּכְתָבָהּ וְעַם וָעָם כִּלְשׁוֹנוֹ: בְּשֵׁם הַמֶּלֶךְ אֲחַשְׁוֵרֹשׁ נִכְתָּב, וְנֶחְתָּם בְּטַבַּעַת הַמֶּלֶךְ.

יג וְנִשְׁלוֹחַ סְפָרִים בְּיַד הָרָצִים, אֶל-כָּל-מְדִינוֹת הַמֶּלֶךְ--לְהַשְׁמִיד לַהֲרֹג וּלְאַבֵּד אֶת-כָּל-הַיְּהוּדִים מִנַּעַר וְעַד-זָקֵן טַף וְנָשִׁים בְּיוֹם אֶחָד, בִּשְׁלוֹשָׁה עָשָׂר לְחֹדֶשׁ שְׁנֵים-עָשָׂר הוּא-חֹדֶשׁ אֲדָר; וּשְׁלָלָם, לָבוֹז.

יד פַּתְשֶׁגֶן הַכְּתָב, לְהִנָּתֵן דָּת בְּכָל-מְדִינָה וּמְדִינָה, גָּלוּי לְכָל-הָעַמִּים--לִהְיוֹת עֲתִדִים, לַיּוֹם הַזֶּה.

טו הָרָצִים יָצְאוּ דְחוּפִים, בִּדְבַר הַמֶּלֶךְ, וְהַדָּת נִתְּנָה, בְּשׁוּשַׁן הַבִּירָה; וְהַמֶּלֶךְ וְהָמָן יָשְׁבוּ לִשְׁתּוֹת, וְהָעִיר שׁוּשָׁן נָבוֹכָה.

Esther Chapter 4

א וּמָרְדֳּכַי, יָדַע אֶת-כָּל-אֲשֶׁר נַעֲשָׂה, וַיִּקְרַע מָרְדֳּכַי אֶת-בְּגָדָיו, וַיִּלְבַּשׁ שַׂק וָאֵפֶר; וַיֵּצֵא בְּתוֹךְ הָעִיר, וַיִּזְעַק זְעָקָה גְדוֹלָה וּמָרָה.

ב וַיָּבוֹא, עַד לִפְנֵי שַׁעַר-הַמֶּלֶךְ: כִּי אֵין לָבוֹא אֶל-שַׁעַר הַמֶּלֶךְ, בִּלְבוּשׁ שָׂק.

ג וּבְכָל-מְדִינָה וּמְדִינָה, מְקוֹם אֲשֶׁר דְּבַר-הַמֶּלֶךְ וְדָתוֹ מַגִּיעַ--אֵבֶל גָּדוֹל לַיְּהוּדִים, וְצוֹם וּבְכִי וּמִסְפֵּד; שַׂק וָאֵפֶר, יֻצַּע לָרַבִּים.

ד וַתָּבוֹאינה (וַתָּבוֹאנָה) נַעֲרוֹת אֶסְתֵּר וְסָרִיסֶיהָ, וַיַּגִּידוּ לָהּ, וַתִּתְחַלְחַל הַמַּלְכָּה, מְאֹד; וַתִּשְׁלַח בְּגָדִים לְהַלְבִּישׁ אֶת-מָרְדֳּכַי, וּלְהָסִיר שַׂקּוֹ מֵעָלָיו--וְלֹא קִבֵּל.

ה וַתִּקְרָא אֶסְתֵּר לַהֲתָךְ מִסָּרִיסֵי הַמֶּלֶךְ, אֲשֶׁר הֶעֱמִיד לְפָנֶיהָ, וַתְּצַוֵּהוּ, עַל-מָרְדֳּכָי--לָדַעַת מַה-זֶּה, וְעַל-מַה-זֶּה.

ו וַיֵּצֵא הֲתָךְ, אֶל-מָרְדֳּכָי--אֶל-רְחוֹב הָעִיר, אֲשֶׁר לִפְנֵי שַׁעַר-הַמֶּלֶךְ.

ז וַיַּגֶּד-לוֹ מָרְדֳּכַי, אֵת כָּל-אֲשֶׁר קָרָהוּ; וְאֵת פָּרָשַׁת הַכֶּסֶף, אֲשֶׁר אָמַר הָמָן לִשְׁקוֹל עַל-גִּנְזֵי הַמֶּלֶךְ ביהודיים (בַּיְּהוּדִים)--לְאַבְּדָם.

ח וְאֶת-פַּתְשֶׁגֶן כְּתָב-הַדָּת אֲשֶׁר-נִתַּן בְּשׁוּשָׁן לְהַשְׁמִידָם, נָתַן לוֹ--לְהַרְאוֹת אֶת-אֶסְתֵּר, וּלְהַגִּיד לָהּ; וּלְצַוּוֹת עָלֶיהָ, לָבוֹא אֶל-הַמֶּלֶךְ לְהִתְחַנֶּן-לוֹ וּלְבַקֵּשׁ מִלְּפָנָיו--עַל-עַמָּהּ.

ט וַיָּבוֹא, הֲתָךְ; וַיַּגֵּד לְאֶסְתֵּר, אֵת דִּבְרֵי מָרְדֳּכָי.

י וַתֹּאמֶר אֶסְתֵּר לַהֲתָךְ, וַתְּצַוֵּהוּ אֶל-מָרְדֳּכָי.

יא כָּל-עַבְדֵי הַמֶּלֶךְ וְעַם-מְדִינוֹת הַמֶּלֶךְ יֹדְעִים, אֲשֶׁר כָּל-אִישׁ וְאִשָּׁה אֲשֶׁר יָבוֹא-אֶל-הַמֶּלֶךְ אֶל-הֶחָצֵר הַפְּנִימִית אֲשֶׁר לֹא-יִקָּרֵא אַחַת דָּתוֹ לְהָמִית, לְבַד

מֵאֲשֶׁר יוֹשִׁיט-לוֹ הַמֶּלֶךְ אֶת-שַׁרְבִיט הַזָּהָב, וְחָיָה, וַאֲנִי, לֹא נִקְרֵאתִי לָבוֹא אֶל-הַמֶּלֶךְ--זֶה, שְׁלוֹשִׁים יוֹם.

יב וַיַּגִּידוּ לְמָרְדֳּכָי, אֵת דִּבְרֵי אֶסְתֵּר.

יג וַיֹּאמֶר מָרְדֳּכַי, לְהָשִׁיב אֶל-אֶסְתֵּר: אַל-תְּדַמִּי בְנַפְשֵׁךְ, לְהִמָּלֵט בֵּית-הַמֶּלֶךְ מִכָּל-הַיְּהוּדִים.

יד כִּי אִם-הַחֲרֵשׁ תַּחֲרִישִׁי, בָּעֵת הַזֹּאת--רֶוַח וְהַצָּלָה יַעֲמוֹד לַיְּהוּדִים מִמָּקוֹם אַחֵר, וְאַתְּ וּבֵית-אָבִיךְ תֹּאבֵדוּ; וּמִי יוֹדֵעַ--אִם-לְעֵת כָּזֹאת, הִגַּעַתְּ לַמַּלְכוּת.

טו וַתֹּאמֶר אֶסְתֵּר, לְהָשִׁיב אֶל-מָרְדֳּכָי.

טז לֵךְ כְּנוֹס אֶת-כָּל-הַיְּהוּדִים הַנִּמְצְאִים בְּשׁוּשָׁן, וְצוּמוּ עָלַי וְאַל-תֹּאכְלוּ וְאַל-תִּשְׁתּוּ שְׁלֹשֶׁת יָמִים לַיְלָה וָיוֹם--גַּם-אֲנִי וְנַעֲרֹתַי, אָצוּם כֵּן; וּבְכֵן אָבוֹא אֶל-הַמֶּלֶךְ, אֲשֶׁר לֹא-כַדָּת, וְכַאֲשֶׁר אָבַדְתִּי, אָבָדְתִּי.

יז וַיַּעֲבֹר, מָרְדֳּכָי; וַיַּעַשׂ, כְּכֹל אֲשֶׁר-צִוְּתָה עָלָיו אֶסְתֵּר.

Esther Chapter 5

א וַיְהִי בַּיּוֹם הַשְּׁלִישִׁי, וַתִּלְבַּשׁ אֶסְתֵּר מַלְכוּת, וַתַּעֲמֹד בַּחֲצַר בֵּית-הַמֶּלֶךְ הַפְּנִימִית, נֹכַח בֵּית הַמֶּלֶךְ; וְהַמֶּלֶךְ יוֹשֵׁב עַל-כִּסֵּא מַלְכוּתוֹ, בְּבֵית הַמַּלְכוּת, נֹכַח, פֶּתַח הַבָּיִת.

ב וַיְהִי כִרְאוֹת הַמֶּלֶךְ אֶת-אֶסְתֵּר הַמַּלְכָּה, עֹמֶדֶת בֶּחָצֵר--נָשְׂאָה חֵן, בְּעֵינָיו; וַיּוֹשֶׁט הַמֶּלֶךְ לְאֶסְתֵּר, אֶת-שַׁרְבִיט הַזָּהָב אֲשֶׁר בְּיָדוֹ, וַתִּקְרַב אֶסְתֵּר, וַתִּגַּע בְּרֹאשׁ הַשַּׁרְבִיט.

ג וַיֹּאמֶר לָהּ הַמֶּלֶךְ, מַה-לָּךְ אֶסְתֵּר הַמַּלְכָּה; וּמַה-בַּקָּשָׁתֵךְ עַד-חֲצִי הַמַּלְכוּת, וְיִנָּתֵן לָךְ.

ד וַתֹּאמֶר אֶסְתֵּר, אִם-עַל-הַמֶּלֶךְ טוֹב--יָבוֹא הַמֶּלֶךְ וְהָמָן הַיּוֹם, אֶל-הַמִּשְׁתֶּה אֲשֶׁר-עָשִׂיתִי לוֹ.

ה וַיֹּאמֶר הַמֶּלֶךְ--מַהֲרוּ אֶת-הָמָן, לַעֲשׂוֹת אֶת-דְּבַר אֶסְתֵּר; וַיָּבֹא הַמֶּלֶךְ וְהָמָן, אֶל-הַמִּשְׁתֶּה אֲשֶׁר-עָשְׂתָה אֶסְתֵּר.

ו וַיֹּאמֶר הַמֶּלֶךְ לְאֶסְתֵּר בְּמִשְׁתֵּה הַיַּיִן, מַה-שְּׁאֵלָתֵךְ וְיִנָּתֵן לָךְ; וּמַה-בַּקָּשָׁתֵךְ עַד-חֲצִי הַמַּלְכוּת, וְתֵעָשׂ.

ז וַתַּעַן אֶסְתֵּר, וַתֹּאמַר: שְׁאֵלָתִי, וּבַקָּשָׁתִי.

ח אִם-מָצָאתִי חֵן בְּעֵינֵי הַמֶּלֶךְ, וְאִם-עַל-הַמֶּלֶךְ טוֹב, לָתֵת אֶת-שְׁאֵלָתִי, וְלַעֲשׂוֹת אֶת-בַּקָּשָׁתִי--יָבוֹא הַמֶּלֶךְ וְהָמָן, אֶל-הַמִּשְׁתֶּה אֲשֶׁר אֶעֱשֶׂה לָהֶם, וּמָחָר אֶעֱשֶׂה, כִּדְבַר הַמֶּלֶךְ.

ט וַיֵּצֵא הָמָן בַּיּוֹם הַהוּא, שָׂמֵחַ וְטוֹב לֵב; וְכִרְאוֹת הָמָן אֶת-מָרְדֳּכַי בְּשַׁעַר הַמֶּלֶךְ, וְלֹא-קָם וְלֹא-זָע מִמֶּנּוּ--וַיִּמָּלֵא הָמָן עַל-מָרְדֳּכַי חֵמָה.

י וַיִּתְאַפַּק הָמָן, וַיָּבוֹא אֶל-בֵּיתוֹ; וַיִּשְׁלַח וַיָּבֵא אֶת-אֹהֲבָיו, וְאֶת-זֶרֶשׁ אִשְׁתּוֹ.

יא וַיְסַפֵּר לָהֶם הָמָן אֶת-כְּבוֹד עָשְׁרוֹ, וְרֹב בָּנָיו; וְאֵת כָּל-אֲשֶׁר גִּדְּלוֹ הַמֶּלֶךְ וְאֵת אֲשֶׁר נִשְּׂאוֹ, עַל-הַשָּׂרִים וְעַבְדֵי הַמֶּלֶךְ.

יב וַיֹּאמֶר, הָמָן--אַף לֹא-הֵבִיאָה אֶסְתֵּר הַמַּלְכָּה עִם-הַמֶּלֶךְ אֶל-הַמִּשְׁתֶּה אֲשֶׁר-עָשָׂתָה, כִּי אִם-אוֹתִי; וְגַם-לְמָחָר אֲנִי קָרוּא-לָהּ, עִם-הַמֶּלֶךְ.

יג וְכָל-זֶה, אֵינֶנּוּ שֹׁוֶה לִי: בְּכָל-עֵת, אֲשֶׁר אֲנִי רֹאֶה אֶת-מָרְדֳּכַי הַיְּהוּדִי--יוֹשֵׁב, בְּשַׁעַר הַמֶּלֶךְ.

יד וַתֹּאמֶר לוֹ זֶרֶשׁ אִשְׁתּוֹ וְכָל-אֹהֲבָיו, יַעֲשׂוּ-עֵץ גָּבֹהַּ חֲמִשִּׁים אַמָּה, וּבַבֹּקֶר אֱמֹר לַמֶּלֶךְ וְיִתְלוּ אֶת-מָרְדֳּכַי עָלָיו, וּבֹא-עִם-הַמֶּלֶךְ אֶל-הַמִּשְׁתֶּה שָׂמֵחַ; וַיִּיטַב הַדָּבָר לִפְנֵי הָמָן, וַיַּעַשׂ הָעֵץ.

Esther Chapter 6

א בַּלַּיְלָה הַהוּא, נָדְדָה שְׁנַת הַמֶּלֶךְ; וַיֹּאמֶר, לְהָבִיא אֶת-סֵפֶר הַזִּכְרֹנוֹת דִּבְרֵי הַיָּמִים, וַיִּהְיוּ נִקְרָאִים, לִפְנֵי הַמֶּלֶךְ.

ב וַיִּמָּצֵא כָתוּב, אֲשֶׁר הִגִּיד מָרְדֳּכַי עַל-בִּגְתָנָא וָתֶרֶשׁ שְׁנֵי סָרִיסֵי הַמֶּלֶךְ--מִשֹּׁמְרֵי, הַסַּף: אֲשֶׁר בִּקְשׁוּ לִשְׁלֹחַ יָד, בַּמֶּלֶךְ אֲחַשְׁוֵרוֹשׁ.

ג וַיֹּאמֶר הַמֶּלֶךְ--מַה-נַּעֲשָׂה יְקָר וּגְדוּלָּה לְמָרְדֳּכַי, עַל-
זֶה; וַיֹּאמְרוּ נַעֲרֵי הַמֶּלֶךְ, מְשָׁרְתָיו, לֹא-נַעֲשָׂה עִמּוֹ,
דָּבָר.

ד וַיֹּאמֶר הַמֶּלֶךְ, מִי בֶחָצֵר; וְהָמָן בָּא, לַחֲצַר בֵּית-
הַמֶּלֶךְ הַחִיצוֹנָה, לֵאמֹר לַמֶּלֶךְ, לִתְלוֹת אֶת-מָרְדֳּכַי עַל-
הָעֵץ אֲשֶׁר-הֵכִין לוֹ.

ה וַיֹּאמְרוּ נַעֲרֵי הַמֶּלֶךְ, אֵלָיו--הִנֵּה הָמָן, עֹמֵד בֶּחָצֵר;
וַיֹּאמֶר הַמֶּלֶךְ, יָבוֹא.

ו וַיָּבוֹא, הָמָן, וַיֹּאמֶר לוֹ הַמֶּלֶךְ, מַה-לַעֲשׂוֹת בָּאִישׁ
אֲשֶׁר הַמֶּלֶךְ חָפֵץ בִּיקָרוֹ; וַיֹּאמֶר הָמָן, בְּלִבּוֹ, לְמִי
יַחְפֹּץ הַמֶּלֶךְ לַעֲשׂוֹת יְקָר, יוֹתֵר מִמֶּנִּי.

ז וַיֹּאמֶר הָמָן, אֶל-הַמֶּלֶךְ: אִישׁ, אֲשֶׁר הַמֶּלֶךְ חָפֵץ
בִּיקָרוֹ.

ח יָבִיאוּ לְבוּשׁ מַלְכוּת, אֲשֶׁר לָבַשׁ-בּוֹ הַמֶּלֶךְ; וְסוּס,
אֲשֶׁר רָכַב עָלָיו הַמֶּלֶךְ, וַאֲשֶׁר נִתַּן כֶּתֶר מַלְכוּת,
בְּרֹאשׁוֹ.

ט וְנָתוֹן הַלְּבוּשׁ וְהַסּוּס, עַל-יַד-אִישׁ מִשָּׂרֵי הַמֶּלֶךְ
הַפַּרְתְּמִים, וְהִלְבִּישׁוּ אֶת-הָאִישׁ, אֲשֶׁר הַמֶּלֶךְ חָפֵץ
בִּיקָרוֹ; וְהִרְכִּיבֻהוּ עַל-הַסּוּס, בִּרְחוֹב הָעִיר, וְקָרְאוּ
לְפָנָיו, כָּכָה יֵעָשֶׂה לָאִישׁ אֲשֶׁר הַמֶּלֶךְ חָפֵץ בִּיקָרוֹ.

י וַיֹּאמֶר הַמֶּלֶךְ לְהָמָן, מַהֵר קַח אֶת-הַלְּבוּשׁ וְאֶת-
הַסּוּס כַּאֲשֶׁר דִּבַּרְתָּ, וַעֲשֵׂה-כֵן לְמָרְדֳּכַי הַיְּהוּדִי, הַיּוֹשֵׁב
בְּשַׁעַר הַמֶּלֶךְ: אַל-תַּפֵּל דָּבָר, מִכֹּל אֲשֶׁר דִּבַּרְתָּ.

יא וַיִּקַּח הָמָן אֶת-הַלְּבוּשׁ וְאֶת-הַסּוּס, וַיַּלְבֵּשׁ אֶת-מָרְדֳּכָי; וַיַּרְכִּיבֵהוּ, בִּרְחוֹב הָעִיר, וַיִּקְרָא לְפָנָיו, כָּכָה יֵעָשֶׂה לָאִישׁ אֲשֶׁר הַמֶּלֶךְ חָפֵץ בִּיקָרוֹ.

יב וַיָּשָׁב מָרְדֳּכַי, אֶל-שַׁעַר הַמֶּלֶךְ; וְהָמָן נִדְחַף אֶל-בֵּיתוֹ, אָבֵל וַחֲפוּי רֹאשׁ.

יג וַיְסַפֵּר הָמָן לְזֶרֶשׁ אִשְׁתּוֹ, וּלְכָל-אֹהֲבָיו, אֵת, כָּל-אֲשֶׁר קָרָהוּ; וַיֹּאמְרוּ לוֹ חֲכָמָיו וְזֶרֶשׁ אִשְׁתּוֹ, אִם מִזֶּרַע הַיְּהוּדִים מָרְדֳּכַי אֲשֶׁר הַחִלּוֹתָ לִנְפֹּל לְפָנָיו לֹא-תוּכַל לוֹ--כִּי-נָפוֹל תִּפּוֹל, לְפָנָיו.

יד עוֹדָם מְדַבְּרִים עִמּוֹ, וְסָרִיסֵי הַמֶּלֶךְ הִגִּיעוּ; וַיַּבְהִלוּ לְהָבִיא אֶת-הָמָן, אֶל-הַמִּשְׁתֶּה אֲשֶׁר-עָשְׂתָה אֶסְתֵּר.

Esther Chapter 7

א וַיָּבֹא הַמֶּלֶךְ וְהָמָן, לִשְׁתּוֹת עִם-אֶסְתֵּר הַמַּלְכָּה.

ב וַיֹּאמֶר הַמֶּלֶךְ לְאֶסְתֵּר גַּם בַּיּוֹם הַשֵּׁנִי, בְּמִשְׁתֵּה הַיַּיִן--מַה-שְּׁאֵלָתֵךְ אֶסְתֵּר הַמַּלְכָּה, וְתִנָּתֵן לָךְ; וּמַה-בַּקָּשָׁתֵךְ עַד-חֲצִי הַמַּלְכוּת, וְתֵעָשׂ.

ג וַתַּעַן אֶסְתֵּר הַמַּלְכָּה, וַתֹּאמַר--אִם-מָצָאתִי חֵן בְּעֵינֶיךָ הַמֶּלֶךְ, וְאִם-עַל-הַמֶּלֶךְ טוֹב: תִּנָּתֶן-לִי נַפְשִׁי בִּשְׁאֵלָתִי, וְעַמִּי בְּבַקָּשָׁתִי.

ד כִּי נִמְכַּרְנוּ אֲנִי וְעַמִּי, לְהַשְׁמִיד לַהֲרוֹג וּלְאַבֵּד; וְאִלּוּ לַעֲבָדִים וְלִשְׁפָחוֹת נִמְכַּרְנוּ, הֶחֱרַשְׁתִּי--כִּי אֵין הַצָּר שֹׁוֶה, בְּנֵזֶק הַמֶּלֶךְ.

ה וַיֹּאמֶר הַמֶּלֶךְ אֲחַשְׁוֵרוֹשׁ, וַיֹּאמֶר לְאֶסְתֵּר הַמַּלְכָּה: מִי הוּא זֶה וְאֵי-זֶה הוּא, אֲשֶׁר-מְלָאוֹ לִבּוֹ לַעֲשׂוֹת כֵּן.

ו וַתֹּאמֶר אֶסְתֵּר--אִישׁ צַר וְאוֹיֵב, הָמָן הָרָע הַזֶּה; וְהָמָן נִבְעַת, מִלִּפְנֵי הַמֶּלֶךְ וְהַמַּלְכָּה.

ז וְהַמֶּלֶךְ קָם בַּחֲמָתוֹ, מִמִּשְׁתֵּה הַיַּיִן, אֶל-גִּנַּת הַבִּיתָן; וְהָמָן עָמַד, לְבַקֵּשׁ עַל-נַפְשׁוֹ מֵאֶסְתֵּר הַמַּלְכָּה--כִּי רָאָה, כִּי-כָלְתָה אֵלָיו הָרָעָה מֵאֵת הַמֶּלֶךְ.

ח וְהַמֶּלֶךְ שָׁב מִגִּנַּת הַבִּיתָן אֶל-בֵּית מִשְׁתֵּה הַיַּיִן, וְהָמָן נֹפֵל עַל-הַמִּטָּה אֲשֶׁר אֶסְתֵּר עָלֶיהָ, וַיֹּאמֶר הַמֶּלֶךְ, הֲגַם לִכְבּוֹשׁ אֶת-הַמַּלְכָּה עִמִּי בַּבָּיִת; הַדָּבָר, יָצָא מִפִּי הַמֶּלֶךְ, וּפְנֵי הָמָן, חָפוּ.

ט וַיֹּאמֶר חַרְבוֹנָה אֶחָד מִן-הַסָּרִיסִים לִפְנֵי הַמֶּלֶךְ, גַּם הִנֵּה-הָעֵץ אֲשֶׁר-עָשָׂה הָמָן לְמָרְדֳּכַי אֲשֶׁר דִּבֶּר-טוֹב עַל-הַמֶּלֶךְ עֹמֵד בְּבֵית הָמָן--גָּבֹהַּ, חֲמִשִּׁים אַמָּה; וַיֹּאמֶר הַמֶּלֶךְ, תְּלֻהוּ עָלָיו.

י וַיִּתְלוּ, אֶת-הָמָן, עַל-הָעֵץ, אֲשֶׁר-הֵכִין לְמָרְדֳּכָי; וַחֲמַת הַמֶּלֶךְ, שָׁכָכָה.

Esther Chapter 8

א בַּיּוֹם הַהוּא, נָתַן הַמֶּלֶךְ אֲחַשְׁוֵרוֹשׁ לְאֶסְתֵּר הַמַּלְכָּה, אֶת-בֵּית הָמָן, צֹרֵר הַיְּהוּדִים (הַיְּהוּדִים); וּמָרְדֳּכַי, בָּא לִפְנֵי הַמֶּלֶךְ--כִּי-הִגִּידָה אֶסְתֵּר, מַה הוּא-לָהּ.

ב וַיָּסַר הַמֶּלֶךְ אֶת-טַבַּעְתּוֹ, אֲשֶׁר הֶעֱבִיר מֵהָמָן, וַיִּתְּנָהּ, לְמָרְדֳּכָי; וַתָּשֶׂם אֶסְתֵּר אֶת-מָרְדֳּכַי, עַל-בֵּית הָמָן.

ג וַתּוֹסֶף אֶסְתֵּר, וַתְּדַבֵּר לִפְנֵי הַמֶּלֶךְ, וַתִּפֹּל, לִפְנֵי רַגְלָיו; וַתֵּבְךְּ וַתִּתְחַנֶּן-לוֹ, לְהַעֲבִיר אֶת-רָעַת הָמָן הָאֲגָגִי, וְאֵת מַחֲשַׁבְתּוֹ, אֲשֶׁר חָשַׁב עַל-הַיְּהוּדִים.

ד וַיּוֹשֶׁט הַמֶּלֶךְ לְאֶסְתֵּר, אֵת שַׁרְבִט הַזָּהָב; וַתָּקָם אֶסְתֵּר, וַתַּעֲמֹד לִפְנֵי הַמֶּלֶךְ.

ה וַתֹּאמֶר אִם-עַל-הַמֶּלֶךְ טוֹב וְאִם-מָצָאתִי חֵן לְפָנָיו, וְכָשֵׁר הַדָּבָר לִפְנֵי הַמֶּלֶךְ, וְטוֹבָה אֲנִי, בְּעֵינָיו--יִכָּתֵב לְהָשִׁיב אֶת-הַסְּפָרִים, מַחֲשֶׁבֶת הָמָן בֶּן-הַמְּדָתָא הָאֲגָגִי, אֲשֶׁר כָּתַב לְאַבֵּד אֶת-הַיְּהוּדִים, אֲשֶׁר בְּכָל-מְדִינוֹת הַמֶּלֶךְ.

ו כִּי אֵיכָכָה אוּכַל, וְרָאִיתִי, בָּרָעָה, אֲשֶׁר-יִמְצָא אֶת-עַמִּי; וְאֵיכָכָה אוּכַל וְרָאִיתִי, בְּאָבְדַן מוֹלַדְתִּי.

ז וַיֹּאמֶר הַמֶּלֶךְ אֲחַשְׁוֵרוֹשׁ לְאֶסְתֵּר הַמַּלְכָּה, וּלְמָרְדֳּכַי הַיְּהוּדִי: הִנֵּה בֵית-הָמָן נָתַתִּי לְאֶסְתֵּר, וְאֹתוֹ תָּלוּ עַל-הָעֵץ--עַל אֲשֶׁר-שָׁלַח יָדוֹ, בַּיְּהוּדִים (בַּיְּהוּדִים).

ח וְאַתֶּם כִּתְבוּ עַל-הַיְּהוּדִים כַּטּוֹב בְּעֵינֵיכֶם, בְּשֵׁם הַמֶּלֶךְ, וְחִתְמוּ, בְּטַבַּעַת הַמֶּלֶךְ: כִּי-כְתָב אֲשֶׁר-נִכְתָּב בְּשֵׁם-הַמֶּלֶךְ, וְנַחְתּוֹם בְּטַבַּעַת הַמֶּלֶךְ--אֵין לְהָשִׁיב.

ט וַיִּקָּרְאוּ סֹפְרֵי-הַמֶּלֶךְ בָּעֵת-הַהִיא בַּחֹדֶשׁ הַשְּׁלִישִׁי הוּא-חֹדֶשׁ סִיוָן, בִּשְׁלוֹשָׁה וְעֶשְׂרִים בּוֹ, וַיִּכָּתֵב כְּכָל-אֲשֶׁר-צִוָּה מָרְדֳּכַי אֶל-הַיְּהוּדִים וְאֶל הָאֲחַשְׁדַּרְפְּנִים-וְהַפַּחוֹת וְשָׂרֵי הַמְּדִינוֹת אֲשֶׁר מֵהֹדּוּ וְעַד-כּוּשׁ שֶׁבַע וְעֶשְׂרִים וּמֵאָה מְדִינָה, מְדִינָה וּמְדִינָה כִּכְתָבָהּ וְעַם וָעָם כִּלְשֹׁנוֹ; וְאֶל-הַיְּהוּדִים--כִּכְתָבָם, וְכִלְשׁוֹנָם.

י וַיִּכְתֹּב, בְּשֵׁם הַמֶּלֶךְ אֲחַשְׁוֵרֹשׁ, וַיַּחְתֹּם, בְּטַבַּעַת הַמֶּלֶךְ; וַיִּשְׁלַח סְפָרִים בְּיַד הָרָצִים בַּסּוּסִים רֹכְבֵי הָרֶכֶשׁ, הָאֲחַשְׁתְּרָנִים--בְּנֵי, הָרַמָּכִים.

יא אֲשֶׁר נָתַן הַמֶּלֶךְ לַיְּהוּדִים אֲשֶׁר בְּכָל-עִיר-וָעִיר, לְהִקָּהֵל וְלַעֲמֹד עַל-נַפְשָׁם--לְהַשְׁמִיד וְלַהֲרֹג וּלְאַבֵּד אֶת-כָּל-חֵיל עַם וּמְדִינָה הַצָּרִים אֹתָם, טַף וְנָשִׁים; וּשְׁלָלָם, לָבוֹז.

יב בְּיוֹם אֶחָד, בְּכָל-מְדִינוֹת הַמֶּלֶךְ אֲחַשְׁוֵרוֹשׁ--בִּשְׁלוֹשָׁה עָשָׂר לְחֹדֶשׁ שְׁנֵים-עָשָׂר, הוּא-חֹדֶשׁ אֲדָר.

יג פַּתְשֶׁגֶן הַכְּתָב, לְהִנָּתֵן דָּת בְּכָל-מְדִינָה וּמְדִינָה, גָּלוּי, לְכָל-הָעַמִּים; וְלִהְיוֹת היהודיים (הַיְּהוּדִים) עתודים (עֲתִידִים) לַיּוֹם הַזֶּה, לְהִנָּקֵם מֵאֹיְבֵיהֶם.

יד הָרָצִים רֹכְבֵי הָרֶכֶשׁ, הָאֲחַשְׁתְּרָנִים, יָצְאוּ מְבֹהָלִים וּדְחוּפִים, בִּדְבַר הַמֶּלֶךְ; וְהַדָּת נִתְּנָה, בְּשׁוּשַׁן הַבִּירָה.

טו וּמָרְדֳּכַי יָצָא מִלִּפְנֵי הַמֶּלֶךְ, בִּלְבוּשׁ מַלְכוּת תְּכֵלֶת וָחוּר, וַעֲטֶרֶת זָהָב גְּדוֹלָה, וְתַכְרִיךְ בּוּץ וְאַרְגָּמָן; וְהָעִיר שׁוּשָׁן, צָהֲלָה וְשָׂמֵחָה.

טז לַיְּהוּדִים, הָיְתָה אוֹרָה וְשִׂמְחָה, וְשָׂשֹׂן, וִיקָר.

יז וּבְכָל-מְדִינָה וּמְדִינָה וּבְכָל-עִיר וָעִיר, מְקוֹם אֲשֶׁר דְּבַר-הַמֶּלֶךְ וְדָתוֹ מַגִּיעַ, שִׂמְחָה וְשָׂשׂוֹן לַיְּהוּדִים, מִשְׁתֶּה וְיוֹם טוֹב; וְרַבִּים מֵעַמֵּי הָאָרֶץ, מִתְיַהֲדִים--כִּי-נָפַל פַּחַד-הַיְּהוּדִים, עֲלֵיהֶם.

Esther Chapter 9

א וּבִשְׁנֵים עָשָׂר חֹדֶשׁ הוּא-חֹדֶשׁ אֲדָר, בִּשְׁלוֹשָׁה עָשָׂר יוֹם בּוֹ, אֲשֶׁר הִגִּיעַ דְּבַר-הַמֶּלֶךְ וְדָתוֹ, לְהֵעָשׂוֹת: בַּיּוֹם, אֲשֶׁר שִׂבְּרוּ אֹיְבֵי הַיְּהוּדִים לִשְׁלוֹט בָּהֶם, וְנַהֲפוֹךְ הוּא, אֲשֶׁר יִשְׁלְטוּ הַיְּהוּדִים הֵמָּה בְּשֹׂנְאֵיהֶם.

ב נִקְהֲלוּ הַיְּהוּדִים בְּעָרֵיהֶם, בְּכָל-מְדִינוֹת הַמֶּלֶךְ אֲחַשְׁוֵרוֹשׁ, לִשְׁלֹחַ יָד, בִּמְבַקְשֵׁי רָעָתָם; וְאִישׁ לֹא-עָמַד לִפְנֵיהֶם, כִּי-נָפַל פַּחְדָּם עַל-כָּל-הָעַמִּים.

ג וְכָל-שָׂרֵי הַמְּדִינוֹת וְהָאֲחַשְׁדַּרְפְּנִים וְהַפַּחוֹת, וְעֹשֵׂי הַמְּלָאכָה אֲשֶׁר לַמֶּלֶךְ--מְנַשְּׂאִים, אֶת-הַיְּהוּדִים: כִּי-נָפַל פַּחַד-מָרְדֳּכַי, עֲלֵיהֶם.

ד כִּי-גָדוֹל מָרְדֳּכַי בְּבֵית הַמֶּלֶךְ, וְשָׁמְעוֹ הוֹלֵךְ בְּכָל-הַמְּדִינוֹת: כִּי-הָאִישׁ מָרְדֳּכַי, הוֹלֵךְ וְגָדוֹל.

ה וַיַּכּוּ הַיְּהוּדִים בְּכָל-אֹיְבֵיהֶם, מַכַּת-חֶרֶב וְהֶרֶג וְאַבְדָן; וַיַּעֲשׂוּ בְשֹׂנְאֵיהֶם, כִּרְצוֹנָם.

ו וּבְשׁוּשַׁן הַבִּירָה, הָרְגוּ הַיְּהוּדִים וְאַבֵּד--חֲמֵשׁ מֵאוֹת, אִישׁ.

ז וְאֵת פַּרְשַׁנְדָּתָא וְאֵת דַּלְפוֹן, וְאֵת אַסְפָּתָא.

ח וְאֵת פּוֹרָתָא וְאֵת אֲדַלְיָא, וְאֵת אֲרִידָתָא.

ט וְאֵת פַּרְמַשְׁתָּא וְאֵת אֲרִיסַי, וְאֵת אֲרִידַי וְאֵת וַיְזָתָא.

י עֲשֶׂרֶת בְּנֵי הָמָן בֶּן-הַמְּדָתָא, צֹרֵר הַיְּהוּדִים--הָרָגוּ; וּבַבִּזָּה--לֹא שָׁלְחוּ, אֶת-יָדָם.

יא בַּיּוֹם הַהוּא, בָּא מִסְפַּר הַהֲרוּגִים בְּשׁוּשַׁן הַבִּירָה--לִפְנֵי הַמֶּלֶךְ.

יב וַיֹּאמֶר הַמֶּלֶךְ לְאֶסְתֵּר הַמַּלְכָּה, בְּשׁוּשַׁן הַבִּירָה הָרְגוּ הַיְּהוּדִים וְאַבֵּד חֲמֵשׁ מֵאוֹת אִישׁ וְאֵת עֲשֶׂרֶת בְּנֵי-הָמָן--בִּשְׁאָר מְדִינוֹת הַמֶּלֶךְ, מֶה עָשׂוּ; וּמַה-שְּׁאֵלָתֵךְ וְיִנָּתֵן לָךְ, וּמַה-בַּקָּשָׁתֵךְ עוֹד וְתֵעָשׂ.

יג וַתֹּאמֶר אֶסְתֵּר, אִם-עַל-הַמֶּלֶךְ טוֹב--יִנָּתֵן גַּם-מָחָר לַיְּהוּדִים אֲשֶׁר בְּשׁוּשָׁן, לַעֲשׂוֹת כְּדָת הַיּוֹם; וְאֵת עֲשֶׂרֶת בְּנֵי-הָמָן, יִתְלוּ עַל-הָעֵץ.

יד וַיֹּאמֶר הַמֶּלֶךְ לְהֵעָשׂוֹת כֵּן, וַתִּנָּתֵן דָּת בְּשׁוּשָׁן; וְאֵת עֲשֶׂרֶת בְּנֵי-הָמָן, תָּלוּ.

טו וַיִּקָּהֲלוּ הַיְּהוּדִיִּים (הַיְּהוּדִים) אֲשֶׁר-בְּשׁוּשָׁן, גַּם בְּיוֹם אַרְבָּעָה עָשָׂר לְחֹדֶשׁ אֲדָר, וַיַּהַרְגוּ בְשׁוּשָׁן, שְׁלֹשׁ מֵאוֹת אִישׁ; וּבַבִּזָּה--לֹא שָׁלְחוּ, אֶת-יָדָם.

טז וּשְׁאָר הַיְּהוּדִים אֲשֶׁר בִּמְדִינוֹת הַמֶּלֶךְ נִקְהֲלוּ וְעָמֹד עַל-נַפְשָׁם, וְנוֹחַ מֵאֹיְבֵיהֶם, וְהָרוֹג בְּשֹׂנְאֵיהֶם, חֲמִשָּׁה וְשִׁבְעִים אָלֶף; וּבַבִּזָּה--לֹא שָׁלְחוּ, אֶת-יָדָם.

יז בְּיוֹם-שְׁלוֹשָׁה עָשָׂר, לְחֹדֶשׁ אֲדָר; וְנוֹחַ, בְּאַרְבָּעָה עָשָׂר בּוֹ, וְעָשֹׂה אֹתוֹ, יוֹם מִשְׁתֶּה וְשִׂמְחָה.

יח וְהַיְּהוּדִיִּים (וְהַיְּהוּדִים) אֲשֶׁר-בְּשׁוּשָׁן, נִקְהֲלוּ בִּשְׁלוֹשָׁה עָשָׂר בּוֹ, וּבְאַרְבָּעָה עָשָׂר, בּוֹ; וְנוֹחַ, בַּחֲמִשָּׁה עָשָׂר בּוֹ, וְעָשֹׂה אֹתוֹ, יוֹם מִשְׁתֶּה וְשִׂמְחָה.

יט עַל-כֵּן הַיְּהוּדִים הפרוזים (הַפְּרָזִים), הַיֹּשְׁבִים בְּעָרֵי הַפְּרָזוֹת--עֹשִׂים אֵת יוֹם אַרְבָּעָה עָשָׂר לְחֹדֶשׁ אֲדָר, שִׂמְחָה וּמִשְׁתֶּה וְיוֹם טוֹב; וּמִשְׁלֹחַ מָנוֹת, אִישׁ לְרֵעֵהוּ.

כ וַיִּכְתֹּב מָרְדֳּכַי, אֶת-הַדְּבָרִים הָאֵלֶּה; וַיִּשְׁלַח סְפָרִים אֶל-כָּל-הַיְּהוּדִים, אֲשֶׁר בְּכָל-מְדִינוֹת הַמֶּלֶךְ אֲחַשְׁוֵרוֹשׁ-- הַקְּרוֹבִים, וְהָרְחוֹקִים.

כא לְקַיֵּם, עֲלֵיהֶם--לִהְיוֹת עֹשִׂים אֵת יוֹם אַרְבָּעָה עָשָׂר לְחֹדֶשׁ אֲדָר, וְאֵת יוֹם-חֲמִשָּׁה עָשָׂר בּוֹ: בְּכָל-שָׁנָה, וְשָׁנָה.

כב כַּיָּמִים, אֲשֶׁר-נָחוּ בָהֶם הַיְּהוּדִים מֵאֹיְבֵיהֶם, וְהַחֹדֶשׁ אֲשֶׁר נֶהְפַּךְ לָהֶם מִיָּגוֹן לְשִׂמְחָה, וּמֵאֵבֶל לְיוֹם

טוֹב; לַעֲשׂוֹת אוֹתָם, יְמֵי מִשְׁתֶּה וְשִׂמְחָה, וּמִשְׁלֹחַ מָנוֹת אִישׁ לְרֵעֵהוּ, וּמַתָּנוֹת לָאֶבְיוֹנִים.

כג וְקִבֵּל, הַיְּהוּדִים, אֵת אֲשֶׁר-הֵחֵלּוּ, לַעֲשׂוֹת; וְאֵת אֲשֶׁר-כָּתַב מָרְדֳּכַי, אֲלֵיהֶם.

כד כִּי הָמָן בֶּן-הַמְּדָתָא הָאֲגָגִי, צֹרֵר כָּל-הַיְּהוּדִים-- חָשַׁב עַל-הַיְּהוּדִים, לְאַבְּדָם; וְהִפִּל פּוּר הוּא הַגּוֹרָל, לְהֻמָּם וּלְאַבְּדָם.

כה וּבְבֹאָהּ, לִפְנֵי הַמֶּלֶךְ, אָמַר עִם-הַסֵּפֶר, יָשׁוּב מַחֲשַׁבְתּוֹ הָרָעָה אֲשֶׁר-חָשַׁב עַל-הַיְּהוּדִים עַל-רֹאשׁוֹ; וְתָלוּ אֹתוֹ וְאֶת-בָּנָיו, עַל-הָעֵץ.

כו עַל-כֵּן קָרְאוּ לַיָּמִים הָאֵלֶּה פוּרִים, עַל-שֵׁם הַפּוּר-- עַל-כֵּן, עַל-כָּל-דִּבְרֵי הָאִגֶּרֶת הַזֹּאת; וּמָה-רָאוּ עַל-כָּכָה, וּמָה הִגִּיעַ אֲלֵיהֶם.

כז קִיְּמוּ וְקִבֵּל (וְקִבְּלוּ) הַיְּהוּדִים עֲלֵיהֶם וְעַל-זַרְעָם וְעַל כָּל-הַנִּלְוִים עֲלֵיהֶם, וְלֹא יַעֲבוֹר--לִהְיוֹת עֹשִׂים אֵת שְׁנֵי הַיָּמִים הָאֵלֶּה, כִּכְתָבָם וְכִזְמַנָּם: בְּכָל-שָׁנָה, וְשָׁנָה.

כח וְהַיָּמִים הָאֵלֶּה נִזְכָּרִים וְנַעֲשִׂים בְּכָל-דּוֹר וָדוֹר, מִשְׁפָּחָה וּמִשְׁפָּחָה, מְדִינָה וּמְדִינָה, וְעִיר וָעִיר; וִימֵי הַפּוּרִים הָאֵלֶּה, לֹא יַעַבְרוּ מִתּוֹךְ הַיְּהוּדִים, וְזִכְרָם, לֹא-יָסוּף מִזַּרְעָם.

כט וַתִּכְתֹּב אֶסְתֵּר הַמַּלְכָּה בַת-אֲבִיחַיִל, וּמָרְדֳּכַי הַיְּהוּדִי--אֶת-כָּל-תֹּקֶף: לְקַיֵּם, אֵת אִגֶּרֶת הַפֻּרִים הַזֹּאת--הַשֵּׁנִית.

ל וַיִּשְׁלַח סְפָרִים אֶל-כָּל-הַיְּהוּדִים, אֶל-שֶׁבַע וְעֶשְׂרִים וּמֵאָה מְדִינָה--מַלְכוּת, אֲחַשְׁוֵרוֹשׁ: דִּבְרֵי שָׁלוֹם, וֶאֱמֶת.

לא לְקַיֵּם אֶת-יְמֵי הַפֻּרִים הָאֵלֶּה בִּזְמַנֵּיהֶם, כַּאֲשֶׁר קִיַּם עֲלֵיהֶם מָרְדֳּכַי הַיְּהוּדִי וְאֶסְתֵּר הַמַּלְכָּה, וְכַאֲשֶׁר קִיְּמוּ עַל-נַפְשָׁם, וְעַל-זַרְעָם: דִּבְרֵי הַצּוֹמוֹת, וְזַעֲקָתָם.

לב וּמַאֲמַר אֶסְתֵּר--קִיַּם, דִּבְרֵי הַפֻּרִים הָאֵלֶּה; וְנִכְתָּב, בַּסֵּפֶר.

Esther Chapter 10

א וַיָּשֶׂם הַמֶּלֶךְ אחשרש (אֲחַשְׁוֵרוֹשׁ) מַס עַל-הָאָרֶץ, וְאִיֵּי הַיָּם.

ב וְכָל-מַעֲשֵׂה תָקְפּוֹ, וּגְבוּרָתוֹ, וּפָרָשַׁת גְּדֻלַּת מָרְדֳּכַי, אֲשֶׁר גִּדְּלוֹ הַמֶּלֶךְ--הֲלוֹא-הֵם כְּתוּבִים, עַל-סֵפֶר דִּבְרֵי הַיָּמִים, לְמַלְכֵי, מָדַי וּפָרָס.

ג כִּי מָרְדֳּכַי הַיְּהוּדִי, מִשְׁנֶה לַמֶּלֶךְ אֲחַשְׁוֵרוֹשׁ, וְגָדוֹל לַיְּהוּדִים, וְרָצוּי לְרֹב אֶחָיו--דֹּרֵשׁ טוֹב לְעַמּוֹ, וְדֹבֵר שָׁלוֹם לְכָל-זַרְעוֹ.

The Blessing After the
Reading of Megillat Esther

According to the Talmud (Tractate Megillah, page 21b), just as a blessing is necessary before the performance of the mitzvah of reading the Megillah, so too is a blessing required after its reading.

What blessing is said after the reading of the Megillah?

"Blessed are you God, King of the Universe, who takes up our grievance, who judges our claim, and who takes revenge for us, and who brings retribution on our enemies. Blessed are you Lord, who exacts vengeance for Israel from its enemies.

The Talmudic sage Rava said that the blessing should end with the words 'The God who brings salvation.' Rav Pappa said that therefore we should say both: Blessed are you, God, who exacts vengeance for Israel from its enemies, the God who brings salvation."

ברוך אתה ה' אלקינו מלך העולם (הא-ל) הרב את ריבנו והדן את דיננו והנוקם את נקמתנו והנפרע לנו מצרינו והמשלם גמול לכל אויבי נפשנו. ברוך אתה ה' הנפרע לישראל מכל צריהם.

רבא אמר: הא-ל המושיע.

אמר רב פפא: הילכך נימרינהו לתרוייהו - ברוך אתה ה' הנפרע לישראל מכל צריהם הא-ל המושיע.

Shoshanat Ya'acov:
A Traditional, Post-Reading Hymn

"The rose [that is] Yaakov was cheerful and glad, when they saw together the royal blue [robes] of Mordechai. You have been their salvation eternally, and their hope throughout generation after generation - to make known that all those who put their hope in You will not be shamed; and they will never be humiliated - all those who take refuge in You. Accursed be Haman, who sought to destroy me; blessed be Mordechai the Jew. Accursed be Zeresh, the wife of my terrorizer; blessed be Esther, who shielded me. And also may Charvona be remembered for good."

שׁוֹשַׁנַּת יַעֲקֹב צָהֲלָה וְשָׂמֵחָה, בִּרְאוֹתָם יַחַד תְּכֵלֶת מָרְדְּכָי, תְּשׁוּעָתָם הָיִיתָ לָנֶצַח, וְתִקְוָתָם בְּכָל דּוֹר וָדוֹר. לְהוֹדִיעַ שֶׁכָּל קֹוֶיךָ לֹא יֵבֹשׁוּ וְלֹא יִכָּלְמוּ לָנֶצַח כָּל הַחוֹסִים בָּךְ. אָרוּר הָמָן אֲשֶׁר בִּקֵּשׁ לְאַבְּדִי, בָּרוּךְ מָרְדְּכָי הַיְּהוּדִי. אֲרוּרָה זֶרֶשׁ אֵשֶׁת מַפְחִידִי, בְּרוּכָה אֶסְתֵּר בַּעֲדִי, אֲרוּרִים כָּל הָרְשָׁעִים, בְּרוּכִים כָּל הַצַּדִּיקִים, וְגַם חַרְבוֹנָה זָכוּר לַטּוֹב:

This medieval song typically follows the reading of the Megillah and ends with the words "and also may Charvonah be remembered for good." The commentary to Chapter 7, verse 9 explains why we honor Charvonah with this praise.

In Rashi's commentary on Esther, he adds that Charvonah emphasizes the degree of Haman's evil in his condemnation of him. After all, Haman had built a gallows on which would hang the man who had once saved the king's life.

But who was Charvona? In Tractate Megilah (16a) we are told that this man was a courtier who was also involved in Haman's plot to kill Mordechai. How else could his knowledge of Haman's plot be explained? We also read in the *Torah Temimah* (a commentary written by 19th century rabbi Baruch Epstein) that he must have been in the company of Haman the night before, actually assisting in the construction of the gallows. It appears that he also knew of the late night reading of the royal chronicles to the king, reminding him of Mordecai's having saved his life. But, providentially, seeing the sudden reversal in fortunes of the Jews, he spoke out against Haman, hastening his downfall.

The song also has a mystical reference.

In the introduction to the *Zohar*, Rabbi Chezkiah said: "It is written: 'As a rose among the thorns, so is my beloved amongst the daughters' (Song of Songs 2:2). Who is the rose? This refers to '*Knesset Yisrael*' - the collective soul roots of Israel . . ." Just as the people of Israel were surrounded by "thorns" in Persia and throughout history, so they were and will always remain the "beloved" of God.

Historical Context, Translation of the Text and Commentary

Introduction

More than 2000 years ago, in the capital city of the Persian Empire, the king celebrated his royal position with a party that lasted for six months. Among his thousands of guests were citizens and officials from every province of his large, multi-ethnic kingdom, including many of his Jewish subjects. What followed was a series of events that nearly led to the destruction of the Jewish people. Only the fortuitous introduction of an unassuming, young Jewish woman to the royal harem averted a disastrous outcome.

The text of the Megillah records a series of very real, historically consistent, seemingly providential twists and turns that resulted in the young woman, Esther, and her uncle and guardian, Mordecai contriving to save the Jews and establish the holiday of Purim.

Why Esther?

A few hundred years before the Common Era, an invasion from the east destroyed the infrastructure and culture of the land of Israel. And while the city of Jerusalem and the Holy Temple were subsequently rebuilt, they never regained their previous spiritual and national stature.

The period between these events was for a very long time something of a physical, spiritual and historical black hole. What became of the Jews who survived the Babylonian conquest and were carried off to Mesopotamia? How did they fare under the Persians, who succeeded the Babylonians and ultimately succumbed to the Greeks?

The origin and historical context of the holiday of Purim is obscured by centuries of cultural and intellectual darkness.

However, over the last century and a half, literary, archaeological and sociological discoveries have turned this formerly little-known time period into a rich and lively canvas populated with iconic personalities, memorable stories and lasting legacies. The texture of Persian life during this era is palpable, and the role of religion is critical. Our protagonists, Mordecai and Esther, are very real people whose actions and both personal and communal desires are predictable and admirable in the light of their unique circumstances. Their fierce attachment to a singular identity as Jews drives them to succeed in both saving their people and insuring the continuity of formal monotheistic faith.

The holiday of Purim has been celebrated for more than 2000 years. In the second book of *Maccabees*, chapter 15, verse 36, the holiday is called Mordecai Day, and 200 years later Josephus records in his *Antiquities of the Jews* that it was commonly celebrated for an entire week.

But acceptance in the ancient world was hardly universal and the *Book of Esther* was not without its critics. In fact, a dispute over its inclusion in the Biblical canon raged for hundreds of years.

The Babylonian Talmud records disagreements concerning the holiday's level of religious inspiration, and includes a statement that many members of the Sanhedrin (the governing, communal religious legal body) in those days separated themselves from Mordecai because of his somewhat less rigorous religious conduct (Tractate Megillah, page 16b). The Babylonian Talmud also records that Esther asked the sages of her time to record the story, but that they refused. Later sages insisted, due to the book's questionable religious character, that it should never have been written down at all, and should have been excluded from the Biblical canon (Tractate Megillah, 7a).

Objections were also voiced in the Jerusalem Talmud as well where it is stated that 85 elders (among them 30 prophets) objected to the observance of the holiday of Purim (this, at least 4 centuries after its establishment). The "Al Hanissim" addition to the daily, Jewish prayer liturgy further demonstrates how the Jewish sages came to grips with this ambivalence. Both the holidays of Purim and Chanukah acknowledge watershed events in the history and continuity of the Jewish people. Yet a side-by-side comparison of these two insertions into the daily Amidah prayer and the grace after meals highlights the narrow, particularist claim of Divine deliverance for the Jews at Purim with the global, Divine revelation associated with Chanukah.

Despite this formal ambivalence, the historical significance of the events recorded in the *Book of Esther* could not be minimized. As a result, efforts to exclude it from the canon failed and its chronological home and inspirational content are included in *Seder Olam* (a rabbinic text dating to the second century of the Common Era, held as the official Biblical Jewish chronology). And to smooth its acceptance, the book's Divine inspiration is highlighted in the Gemara, while Mordecai is variously described as a religious leader and a member of the Anshei Knesset HaGedolah (the pre-common era council of 120 great Torah sages).

In stark contrast to the canonical treatment of the Purim story, is that of Chanukah. *Maccabees I and II* tell a story that smacks of "overt" divine intervention and inspiration, took place in the Holy Land and resulted in the survival of traditional religious practice as well as the holiday of Chanukah. But, unlike Esther, those books are not included in the Biblical canon – most likely for the simplest of reasons: they came too late. This conclusion is bolstered by the mention of the Hasmonean period as only an afterthought in *Seder Olam*, while Esther is highlighted. In fact *Maccabees II* itself supports the effective "closure" of the Biblical canon before its own writing by recounting Judah Maccabee collecting all of the canonical books in order to preserve them after the Greek king Antiochus had pointedly destroyed all that he could find.

There has been much discussion that among the Dead Sea Scrolls (Second Temple era manuscripts found in the mid-twentieth century in caves near Qumran outside of Jerusalem) were found all of the Jewish canonical texts except Esther. Esther is also absent from the Greek Old Testament of Bishop Melito of Sardis (d. 180 C.E.). While many experts on the Scrolls see this as a chance omission, it is possible that since Purim was not on the Qumran community calendar and that the community was extreme in its religious practices, the source book for this holiday was simply not considered "divine enough" to be part of its canon. Various Christians, including Martin Luther later echoed this view in excoriating the *Book of Esther*.

Who Wrote the *Book of Esther?*

There is no ISBN number assigned to the *Book of Esther*, nor is there an original, signed copy. As far as we know, the author never conducted a cross-country promotional tour. So how can we know who wrote a book that has been in our possession for more than two millennia?

Neither the text nor the social context tell us who the author was, but they reveal a good deal about when the author lived and what sort of person he or she may have been.

According to rabbis of the Babylonian Talmud (Tractate Bava Batra, page 15a), the *Book of Esther* was written by Mordecai and then edited and adapted by the pre-common era, Anshei Knesset Hagadolah (the assembly of great sages) before being put into public circulation. This was also the belief of Josephus, the first century soldier-historian and witness to the destruction of Jerusalem by the Romans. It is also posited that either the Biblical characters Ezra or Nechemia may have authored the book. But the events may have actually taken place contemporaneously with their lives or after their passing.

As is reflected in the commentary to the text below, it is more likely that the author was a Persian Jew, living sometime after the events actually occurred, but very close, both geographically and spiritually to them. The author was very familiar with lay Persian customs and the customs of its monarchy. He was intimate with the geography of Susa/Shushan and the palace itself. And, he was also aware of the existence, content and availability of the Persian royal chronicles.

Perhaps more significant was the author's comfort and familiarity with the language and content of the Torah and the Bible in general. A practicing Jew, albeit, in the days before the structure of the oral law had been fully formulated (which began in the Maccabean period), he or she understood the tension between the practicing and assimilated segments of the Persian Jewish community. The author either shaped the book to reflect personal religious principles or was followed by one or more editors who did so. In the final analysis, the degree of his or her religiosity is a minor issue, since we can imagine that today's definitions of a religious Jew and a secular Jew likely did not apply in Susa 2500 years ago.

What we can be sure of is that by recording these events in just this way, our author intentionally depicted first, the plight of the Jews in a hostile Diaspora setting, next, their providential rescue and finally, their strategic plan to guarantee the continuity of their disparate and scattered community in the face of continued religious oppression.

When did the *Book of Esther* Take Place?

The Confusing Chronology of Ancient History

The conventional dating of ancient history, beginning with the rise of ancient Egypt and ending with the ascension of the Greeks, is likely off by several centuries. Errors, including those born of Sothic dating, the double counting of simultaneously reigning monarchs, and kings with multiple names and titles have contributed to the accepted, but erroneous ancient Egyptian chronology.

Some of these chronological errors may have crept into the timeline of the Persian period as well. However, as a result of the conventionally accepted timeline, the chronology of the Persian period as recorded in *Seder Olam* and the Bible is routinely dismissed by historians, most of the rishonim (Biblical commentators of the early Middle Ages) and almost all of the acharonim (later commentators).

According to *Seder Olam* the Second Temple stood in Jerusalem for 420 years and was destroyed in the year 70 CE by the Romans. But before that, a period of 70 years elapsed between the destruction of the First Temple by the Babylonians and the commencement of its rebuilding under Persian rule. So Jewish tradition and history calculate that the destruction of the first Temple occurred in 421/2 BCE, not in 586/7 as all 19th and 20th century historians have burned into our collective consciousness.

The conventional chronology of the Persian period of ancient history owes its existence primarily to the writings of Herodotus, Plutarch, Ctesias and other ancient Greek historians who reassembled Persian history from observation and anecdotal evidence. In doing so, they accounted for 10 kings. Josephus in his *Antiquities* counts six while the Bible, as represented by the *Book of Daniel* accounts for only four – the number and identities of whom were subsequently adopted by *Seder Olam*.

Jewish/Daniel Kings List	Conventional/ Persian List
Darius the Mede (369BCE)	Cyrus (560-530BCE)
Cyrus the Great (369-366)	Cambyses (530-522)
Achashverosh (366-352)	(Guamata the Magian (522)usurper)
Darius the Persian (352-317)	Darius I (522-486)
	Xerxes I (486-455)
	Artaxerxes I (465-424)
	Darius II (424-405)
	Artaxerxes II (405-359)
	Artaxerxes III (359-338)
	Arses (338-336)
	Darius III (336-331) Defeated by Alexander

So, in summary, according to conventional historians,

➤ The Babylonian Empire was established by Nabopolassar and his son, Nebuchadnezzar about 605 BCE, following the battle of Karkemish, or slightly earlier following the fall of Nineveh and the Assyrian Empire. Nebuchadnezzar destroyed Jerusalem in 586/7 BCE.

➤ The Babylonian Empire was destroyed by the Persian king Cyrus in 539 BCE.

➤ The Persian Empire established by Cyrus was destroyed by Alexander the Grect in 331 BCE, following the Battle of Gaugamela. The Persian Empire lasted for 208 years.

While, according to Seder Olam following the Biblical texts,

> ➢ Nabopolassar and Nebuchadnezzar established the Babylonian Empire in 433 BCE (assuming that the Battle of Karkemish is the watershed event at this point in the history of the Middle East).

> ➢ Nebuchadnezzar destroyed Jerusalem in 422 BCE.

> ➢ In 370 BCE, the Median king Darius and his Persian relative Cyrus conquered Babylon and destroyed the Babylonian Empire, establishing their own Medo-Persian Empire (with kings descended from the royal line of Achamaenes). <u>The Persian Empire lasted for 52 years</u> before being conquered by Alexander the Great.

In order for the Jewish timeline to be accurate, some of the kings mentioned in the conventional kings list would have to have been vassal kings, subservient to the four primary kings of the era, or duplications.

Arguments can be made for the validity of both historical accounts, but that conflict does not alter the veracity of the Megillah's narrative.

What to Look for in the Text of Esther

The historical validity of the *Book of Esther* depends on just how comfortably its events fit into the chosen period of ancient history. Recognition and understanding by the reader of three categories of "evidence," the detail for which is found below in the commentary on the Megillah itself, bolsters its historicity:

First, the text contains details that verify the cultural accuracy of the narrative:

- ❖ The king is unable to revoke a royal decree.
- ❖ The king makes important decisions under the influence of alcohol, with advisors present.
- ❖ There is honor associated with wearing a garment formerly worn by the king.

Then, the text presents a sociological picture of the monarchy and its conduct:

- ❖ The harem has extraordinary influence over the king.
- ❖ The royal wife has significant standing among the people and in the royal family.
- ❖ Touching the wife of the king is punishable by death.
- ❖ The actions leading to punishment of a traitor also imply such punishment for his sons.

Finally, historical and archaeological discoveries support the text:

- ❖ There is a detailed description in the text of the palace in Susa/Shushan that has an archaeological twin.
- ❖ Changing religious circumstances form an important backdrop to events.
- ❖ The economic profile of the prime minister's campaign against the Jews is consistent with that of an earlier Persian military campaign.
- ❖ The acquisition of additional territory by this king for his empire is alluded to and historically corroborated.

Historic Lessons of Esther

The Jews of ancient Persia overcame an existential threat in the time of Mordecai and Esther.

It is remarkable that the 21st century's national Islamic successor nation, Iran, demonizes Israel and the Jews for the "holocaust" carried out against the Persians so long ago. The irony that the very existence of Islam can be attributed to the rescue of monotheism by the Jews of that era totally escapes them. But in ancient Persia, the turn of events was so dramatic that, as indicated in the Megillah itself, many gentile bystanders chose to join the Jewish faith.

As is described in the commentary below, Mordecai, Esther and subsequent religious leaders chose the date and some of the activities of the holiday of Purim to insure that they would blend seamlessly with an important pagan holiday of the time. It must have been the intent of the creators of Purim to "hide" the Jewish celebration within a larger Persian celebration to avoid singling out the Jews and risking a repetition of the earlier persecution. The Jews were destined to remain citizens of the Persian Empire for some time after these events, and it was essential that they find a way to observe their own holiday without drawing attention to their separatist practices, including their objection to image worship.

The name, Esther, connotes "hidden" in Hebrew. And commentators have routinely associated that name with the hidden nature of God's providential role in the salvation of the Jewish people. In fact, God is not mentioned even once in the book. Yet, the name Esther may just as accurately be associated with the "hidden" nature of the holiday itself, deliberately subsumed in the customs and activities of a major, pre-existing Persian holiday.

The celebratory activities promoted by Mordecai and Esther, including those held in common with their pagan neighbors (sending both gifts to one another and charity to the needy) appear to have been designed to encourage a strong sense of community in response to the existential threat just survived. Multiple letters from Mordecai and Esther along with a history of ambivalence on the part of religious leaders demonstrate that community building among the religious and the secular was going to be needed if Jewish continuity was to be guaranteed.

"And the Jews confirmed it as a duty and took it upon themselves and their seed . . .and they would celebrate . . . in each and every year." (Esther 9:27) Exiled from their homeland and spreading to every civilized corner of the world, the people of Israel used the events described in the Book of Esther to develop common practices that to this day help to bridge the religious divide.

The Book of Esther, Chapter 1

1 Now it came to pass in the days of Achashverosh--this is Achashverosh who reigned, from India to Ethiopia, over a hundred and twenty seven provinces

Without telling the reader in so many words, the author of the *Book of Esther* offers the contextual information required to place this drama historically. He or she must have lived sometime after these events took place, but while the Jews still lived in Persia under Achamaenian rule.

The author takes for granted that the reader is aware of the fact that there were a number of kings known by the "title" Achashverosh, so it was important that no doubt be left as to the monarch in question. This is done, not through the provision of personal details about the king, but by the offering of a single piece of information that differentiates the reign of this king from that of any other who may have ruled under that name or title.

The Biblical commentator, Avraham Ibn Ezra, who lived in 12th century Spain, wrote two commentaries on the *Book of Esther*, one in Italy and another later in France. In reference to this opening sentence he explained that of all of the kings reigning under this name, this particular Achashverosh had to be the one who reigned over the geographically largest kingdom. If that were not so, he explains, then the author of Esther would not have bothered to enumerate the number of provinces under his rule.

This conclusion contradicts a belief prevalent among many conventional 19th and early 20th century historians. They believed that the king of this particular time period was the one known by Greek historians as Xerxes. But, Greek histories recount that Xerxes lost parts of his kingdom to the Greeks during his reign and as a result ruled over a smaller kingdom than did one of his successors, Artaxerxes II.

Both Jewish and Christian medieval commentators identify the king of the *Book of Esther* with Artaxerxes II, as does Josephus, writing in the first century CE. For example, in a work known as the *Chronicles of Bar Hebraeus* (1250 CE), Bishop Gregory (Bar Hebraeus) says, "this Artaxerxes II the Hebrews call

Achashverosh and therefore Johanan was of the opinion that the story of Esther occurred in his days." In addition, the Greek version of Esther (post-dating the original Hebrew by at least three centuries) incorporated into the Christian canon, identifies Achashverosh with Artaxerxes, not Xerxes.

A Persian account of events is recorded by Masudi in *The Meadows of Gold* (completed 947 CE). He refers to a Jewish woman who had married the Persian King Bahman (Artaxerxes II), and delivered her people.

This larger empire over which the king of our story ruled is described later in the book: "And the king Achashverosh laid a tribute upon the land, *and upon the isles of the sea.*" (Esther 10:1) This not only helps us identify Achashverosh, but it tells us that the expansion of the empire (to the Isles of the Sea) occurred after our protagonist, Mordecai had replaced Haman as prime minister (Chapter 8, verse 2 below).

2 that in those days, when the king Achashverosh sat on the throne of his kingdom, which was in Shushan the capital,

Shushan is known secularly and in both the literature of Greece and archaeology as Susa, one of the major cities of ancient Persia.

The word *bira* -- which in modern Hebrew means "capital (city)"-- meant something different in its Biblical context. Most believe that it is derived from the Akkadian *birtu*, meaning "fortress." The word is found in Nechemiah (1:1, 2:8, 7:2), Chronicles I (29:1,19 where it referred to the Beit HaMikdash/Holy Temple or the fortress protecting it), Daniel (8:2) and often here in Megillat Esther describing Shushan.

Ibn Ezra differentiates the **city** of Shushan from the **bira** of Shushan – a necessary distinction because in Chapter 3:15 and Chapter 8:14-15 both the city and the **bira** are mentioned as if it is understood that these are two independent entities.

What is more, Rabbi Meir Mazuz (a modern Tunisian Sephardic leader with a particular expertise in Hebrew grammar) points out that in the *Book of Esther*, Shushan is always spelled with the vowel *kamatz*, whereas Shushan HaBira is always spelled with the vowel *patach*, further differentiating the two.

3 in the third year of his reign, he made a feast for all his princes and his servants; the army of Persia and Media, the nobles and princes of the provinces, before him;

This seems rather strange. A coronation-like feast was given by the reigning monarch as if to celebrate his ascension to the throne -- *but not until the third year of his reign?* The medieval Biblical commentator, Rashi interprets this as meaning that for the first time during the period of his reign, the kingdom was firmly established as his. If so, then there must have been a rival to this would-be king, who after three years was no longer challenging his royal claim. *One of those named on the conventional Persian kings list, Darius II, battled over the throne with his brother Artaxerxes II and was killed by that brother nearly three years into his reign.*

According to the Biblical thread of history (*remember from the introduction above that the conventional and Biblical timelines are in conflict, as are the number and names of the Persian monarchs*), after the death of Darius the Mede, who conquered Babylon with his nephew/son-in-law Cyrus the Great, there was a battle for the throne between Cyrus and Achashverosh (remember too that we are equating Achashverosh with Artaxerxes II), the son of Darius. *After almost three years, Artaxerxes killed Cyrus and became the undisputed monarch.* In fact, Greek histories record that Artaxerxes arranged for his rival's murder at the Battle of Cunaxa, almost three years after assuming the throne. This is the celebration with which the Megillah opens, and it is consistent with both the conventional and Biblical accounts.

When Darius died, Cyrus (or Darius II according to the conventional chronology), a committed **Zoroastrian** (we will get to Zoroastrianism and its influence in Chapter 3, verse 2), assumed the disputed throne for three years and ordered that the Jews be permitted to return to Zion and rebuild the Temple.

A storehouse of Aramaic papyri, the same variety of Aramaic as that of the Biblical books of Ezra and Nechemia, was found in Egypt and "conventionally" dated to the reign of Darius II of Persia. Coordinating the conflicting historical timelines leaves these documents as having been written during the period shortly before Ezra came to Jerusalem to solidify the community of repatriots there. One letter was sent from Chanani in Judea (who we meet in Nechemia 1:2) to the Egyptian Jewish community in Elephantine (Yev) telling them that King Darius had ordered that the Jews observe the holiday of Passover unmolested (this is recorded on what is known by archaeologists as the Cowley 21 Papyrus now housed in a museum in Berlin).

Unfortunately for the Jews of Persia and Jerusalem, the new king's rival, Achashverosh/Artaxerxes II arranged to have him killed in battle (as described above), and took the throne unchallenged -- hence the celebration.

And it follows that (Ezra 4:6) "And in the days of Achashverosh in the beginning of his reign, they wrote an accusation against the inhabitants of Judea and Jerusalem." As we will see, Achashverosh was about to implement changes in his kingdom that affected daily life in all 127 provinces and resulted in a halt to the reconstruction of the Temple in Jerusalem.

4 when he showed the riches of his kingdom and the honor of his majesty, many days, a hundred and eighty days.

5 And when these days were fulfilled, the king made a feast for all the people that were present in Shushan the castle, both great and small, seven days, in the court of the garden of the king's palace;

The midrash (extra-Biblical commentary and aggadah), Esther Rabbah, relates that 18,500 Jews were invited to the coronation of Achashverosh. And while the historical accuracy of midrashim is often challenged, they are written to make or emphasize important points. This midrash highlights the understanding of later religious commentators that assimilation in ancient Persia was pervasive. Jews were likely prominent in secular circles, both socially and economically.

This may also point once more to the difference between Shushan ha'bira and Shushan. It seems quite a bit more reasonable that "all" of those present in the "palace" or "fortress" were invited to this "garden party" rather than every citizen of the city or officer from the outlying provinces!

6 there were hangings of white, fine cotton, and blue, bordered with cords of fine linen and purple, upon silver rods and pillars of marble; couches of gold and silver, on a floor of green, and white, and shell, and onyx marble.

While Greek historians have given us much of what we know about the kings of Persia, additional information has been gleaned from palace inscriptions uncovered in Persepolis and other major cities.

The French archaeologist, Dieulafoy describes the ruins of Susa (Shushan) in exactly the same terms as are used here. In addition to these materials and furnishings, those ruins carry an engraving identifying the palace as that of Artaxerxes.

Furthermore, his archaeological findings support the distinction between Shushan HaBira and Shushan the city, "This distinguishes the acropolis, in which the palace lay, from the less strongly fortified surrounding city of Susa, which lay on the other side of the river Choaspses." This tells us that not only was the palace separate from the rest of the city but that it was separated from the city by the Biblical Gichon river (Choaspses).

And, Tractate Megillah of the Babylonian Talmud on page 15a tells us that Mordechai crossed a river in order to pass along the message that he had taken from Esther - who was in the *bira* (as we will see below)- to the Jews in the city of Shushan!

7 And they drank in vessels of gold—each of the vessels being different--and royal wine in abundance, according to the generosity of the king.

According to Greek historian Ctesias (in the Greek work, *Athenaei Deipnosoph*), when a king would disgrace a man, he obliged him to use earthen cups. Here, then the use of gold emphasized that every man should feel like a king.

The Targum (an Aramaic translation/interpretation of the Hebrew text) identifies these as the golden vessels of the Holy Temple, removed by Nebuchadnezzar in his conquest of Jerusalem. But this is very problematic since in the Book of Ezra (1:7) we are told that those vessels had been delivered by Cyrus to Zerubbabel who brought them to Jerusalem to be included in the rebuilding of the Holy Temple.

8 And the drinking was according to the law; there was no compulsion; for so the king had directed all the officers of his house, that they should do according to each man's wishes.

Strabo (who lived in Rome at about the turn of the Common Era, and wrote the 17 volume *Geography* -- this reference from volume 15) relates that this very special wine drunk by the kings of Persia was Chalybonian wine, or as Ezekiel Chapter 27:18 calls it, the wine of Chelbon.

Another Greek historian, Xenophon (who lived in Athens during the latter part of the Persian empire, and who was a contemporary of Socrates) wrote in his *The Education of Cyrus* that יין מלכות was wine from the royal cellar -- very expensive wine.

Ernest Bertheau (German Biblical scholar of the 19th century) also remarks that the instructions of the king took into account the drinking habits of even the Jews: "We are not told in the present passage, that the king, on this occasion, exceptionally permitted moderation, especially to such of his guests as were, according to their ancestral customs, addicted to moderation (i.e. the Jews and rigorous Zoroastrians), and who would else have been compelled to drink immoderately. For the words with which this verse concludes, which they imply also a permission to each to drink as little as he chose, are specially intended to allow everyone to take much."

9 Also Vashti the queen made a feast for the women in the royal house which belonged to king Achashverosh.

The Greeks bring yet another historic parallel to the Megillah here. Plutarch (Greek historian of the first century C.E. who while highly critical of Herodotus, was a self-identified expert on the Achamaenian kings) tells of the king being deeply in love with his queen and proud of her beauty. Plutarch calls her a virtuous woman, influential in the palace and with the people.

10 On the seventh day, when the heart of the king was merry with wine, he directed Mehuman, Bizzetha, Harbona, Bigtha, and Abagtha, Zethar, and Carcas, the seven chamberlains that ministered in the presence of Achashverosh the king,

11 to bring Vashti the queen before the king with the royal crown, to show the people and the princes her beauty; for she was beautiful to look at.

The midrashim understand the king to have commanded his queen to appear naked in public, wearing only her crown. Many commentators strive to show that the king wanted to embarrass his wife and minimize her royal status, because, as many historians note, it was she who was of royal birth (from the line of Nebuchadnezzar of Babylon) and not he.

According to the Malbim (Rabbi Meir Loeb ben Yechiel Michael Malbim, a 19th century Russian Bible exegete) being escorted by mere chamberlains rather royal officers was an announcement on the part of the king concerning Vashti's inferior genealogy. Part of demeaning her imperial status involved him sending *his* chamberlains rather than her own.

The language of command also gives a strong hint that Vashti was none too pleased with being asked to make an appearance and in this fashion.

Malbim also makes a distinction between Queen Vashti and Vashti, the Queen. The former construction would imply that she was a product of the royal family, while the later would indicate only her elevation to royal status. In fact we later find Esther addressed in the same manner, as Esther the Queen, not Queen Esther.

12 But the queen Vashti refused to come with the chamberlains at the king's command; and therefore was the king very agitated, and his anger burned within him.

In contrast with the language of verses 9 through 11, here Vashti is called Queen Vashti, not Vashti, the Queen. The queen sees herself as royal born, not raised to that office by virtue of her marriage to the king.

Greek historians recognized that women had an "unnaturally powerful role in the imperial family." (Gene Garthwaite, *The Persians, 2005*) To the well versed in the royal social structure, it comes as no surprise for the queen to have ignored the drunken request of her husband for an embarrassing appearance at the great celebration.

13 Then the king said to the wise men, who knew the times--for so was the king's behavior toward all who knew law and judgment;

These were his trusted and regular advisors who were familiar with his typical behavior, the ambient political circumstances and the law of the land. He also trusted them to be familiar with the doings of the rank and file in his kingdom.

14 and the closest (advisors) to him were Carshena, Shethar, Admatha, Tarshish, Meres, Marsena, and Memucan, the seven princes of Persia and Media, who saw the king's face, and sat (ranking) first in the kingdom:

The sages go to great lengths to equate Memucan with Haman, the villain of the *Book of Esther*. In both midrashim and the Babylonian Talmud – Megillah 12b – it is said that "punishments were prepared (memucan) for him" according to the literal meaning of this alternate name.

As described by three amoraim (rabbis of the Talmud), the prince, Memucan, had a daughter who he longed to have marry into the royal family. For this reason he hated Vashti, the king's wife, and sought to remove her. The rabbis use verse 19 below as the proof text that Memucan/Haman's daughter would be next in line to take Vashti's place. But according to the targum, disfiguring afflictions were visited on Memucan's daughter when she appeared before the king, and Esther emerged from the process as the favorite.

15 What shall we do to the queen Vashti according to law, as she has not done as directed by the king Achashverosh as was to be carried out by the chamberlains?

Tractate Megillah of the Babylonian Talmud describes Vashti as an evil woman who merited this punishment in response to her behavior toward Jewish women. She would force them to work on the Sabbath while naked, and as a result was punished with her husband's command to appear unclothed at his banquet on the Sabbath. This fulfills the principle of having divine retribution match the original crime and is known in Hebrew as "middah k'neged middah" (measure-for-measure).

Tractate Kiddushin (72a) of the Babylonian Talmud describes Babylonian women as having a deep-seated hatred of Jews. Since Vashti was thought to be of noble Babylonian birth, and then married a man who had forcibly taken the Persian throne, it makes sense that she would be presented here in a very negative way.

Despite this midrashic and aggadic tradition, the Jerusalem Talmud offers a very different picture of the Persian queen.

She is seen there as the daughter of royalty (the great granddaughter of Nebuchadnezzar) who behaves in the manner of nobility. n fact, before disobeying the command of her husband to appear at his celebration, she sent her own servants to him on three separate occasions.

She first implored her husband reasoning that, "If your guests see me and think that I am beautiful, they will want to take me for themselves, and they will kill you. And if they see me and think that I am ugly, you will be embarrassed." When that approach failed to elicit a response, she scolded her husband in a second message. "When you were my father's attendant you routinely had naked women appear before you. Now as king, your ways have not changed at all!" Finally, she offered an appeal to his sense of justice saying, "You want me to come unclothed—even my father, when he judged at a trial, would not judge defendants when they were naked!" (Midrash Esther Rabbah 3:14).

Vashti appears wise enough to make appeals to her husband's logic, honor and finally compassion in an attempt to have him reverse his demand. However, the midrash also provides fodder for Vasht's identification with the enemies of Israel. It describes the desire of Achashverosh to rebuild the Temple in Jerusalem and offers Vashti as the principal reason for his not doing so: "You wish to rebuild what my forefathers destroyed?" And, as a result, she was punished by being deposed.

Even though we see some chronological and historical contradictions in this midrashic treatment of Vashti, it is clear that she was a figure of some standing and that rabbinic sages attempted to link her punishment to her mistreatment of the Jews.

16 And Memucan answered before the king and the princes: 'Vashti the queen has not only done wrong to the king, but also to all the princes and to all the people that are in all the provinces of the king Achashverosh.

17 For this deed of the queen will spread to all women, to make their husbands contemptible in their eyes, when it will be said: The king Achashverosh commanded Vashti the queen to be brought before him, but she did not come.

18 And this day will the princesses of Persia and Media who have heard of the deed of the queen say the same to all the king's princes. As a result, there will be contempt and wrath.

The princesses of Persia and Media were witnesses to the event. Memucan emphasized the urgency of action in order to staunch the damage that might be done once word of the queen's obstinacy spread beyond the palace.

19 If it please the king, let there be issued a royal commandment from him, and let it be written among the laws of the Persians and the Medes, that it be not changed, that Vashti will no longer come before king Achashverosh, and that the king will give her royal position to one who is better than she.

To save face, the king acceded to removing from Vashti her rank as queen, but he retained her as his wife. The king was quite fond of Vashti (Plutarch above), and as will be seen in the first verse of Chapter 2, had second thoughts about these actions – actions taken in a drunken state.

Ctesias was a 5th century BCE Greek physician to the Persian court who recorded that the mother of Artaxerxes hated his wife and used this opportunity to murder her. History records that the wife of Artaxerxes II did, in fact die that year.

The midrash corroborates this Greek historical parallel by noting that Vashti is said to have been murdered sometime after embarrassing the king by not appearing at his celebration.

Known for her beauty, this queen is called Statiera by both Plutarch and Ctesias. Vashti in Persian means beauty.

20 And when the king's decree which he shall make throughout all his kingdom, great though it be, all the wives will give honor to their husbands, both to great and small.

21 And this thing was good in the eyes of the king and the princes; and the king did according to the word of Memucan;

Memucan is said by the sages to be Haman. Here, Haman elevates himself above the other advisors to the king. Later, through more strategic advice concerning the security of the kingdom, he becomes Prime Minister, second only to the king himself.

22 and he sent letters to all the king's provinces, into every province according to the writing thereof, and to every people in their (own) language, that every man should be the ruler in his own house, and speak according to the language of his people.

The Persian empire was an agglomeration of ethnicities, each with its own customs, languages, and as we will see later, religions.

Many older commentators explain that the mixture of ethnicities in Persia encouraged intermarriage and so a man often married a woman whose native tongue was different from his own. This decree established that the language of the husband was to be used exclusively in his house.

This contrasts with circumstances found in Judea at this time. There, a foreign wife's native tongue may well have been used in the home (Nechemia 13:23) and as a result Jewish children often could not speak the language of their fathers and ancestors.

Esther Chapter 2

1 After these things, when the anger of king Achashverosh was assuaged, he remembered Vashti, and what she had done, and what was decreed against her.

Vashti was loved by the king, and he regretted deposing her. Later, much to his chagrin, her removal as queen facilitated her murder.

2 the king's servants that ministered to him said to him: 'Let there be sought for the king young virgins fair to look on;

It was imperative that the king be distracted before he acted to restore Vashti to power. She was clearly a thorn in the side of his princes and in particular, Haman/Memucan their leader. Her return would endanger those who had lobbied for her removal and punishment. A search for a replacement was organized without delay.

3 and let the king appoint officers in all the provinces of his kingdom, and they will gather together all the fair young virgins to Shushan the castle, to the house of the women, to the custody of Hegai the king's chamberlain, keeper of the women; and have their ointments given to them;

The harem was a major focus of the king and its keeper occupied an important position. Eduard Meyer, the famous 19th/20th century German historian of antiquity, describes Artaxerxes in the same way that Achashverosh is depicted in the Megillah: good natured, weak, capricious, easily influenced by those close to him and overly influenced by the harem. But he was the only Persian ruler to prevail against the Greeks and expand the Persian empire.

4 and let the maiden that is most pleasing in the eyes of the king be queen instead of Vashti.' And the idea pleased the king; and he did so.

5 There was a Jew in Shushan the castle, whose name was Mordecai the son of Jair the son of Shimei the son of Kish, a Benjamite,

Was Mordecai the only Jew living in Shushan HaBira? Was he providentially in the right place at the right time as the Vilna Gaon (Rabbi Eliayhu Kramer, 18th century Eastern European commentator and religious icon) believed? Or was Mordecai the only Jew in the Palace at Susa because, even before the elevation of Esther, he was a judge in the royal court (per medieval commentator ibn Ezra in his later French commentary on Chapter 1:2)? In any case, it seems that his presence there was very unusual.

The introduction of Mordecai is doubly confusing. Who was carried away with (Judean king) Jeconiah/Jehoiachin in 597 BCE (11 years before the destruction of the Temple and the city of Jerusalem by Nebuchadnezzar, the Babylonian king), Mordecai or Kish?

Many believe that the Kish mentioned here is the father of Saul (the first king of Israel, as recounted in the Book of Samuel). In his commentary, Abraham Ibn Ezra writes that were this so, then the author would certainly have mentioned this fact. If the verse is parsed in one way, then it is Kish who was carried away in 597, not Mordecai. But many other commentators reject this interpretation because of the Masoretic (traditional textual) division which places this clause at the beginning of the following verse (this may have been done by the author or in subsequent revisions to deliberately give the book a more traditionally religious tone).

6 who had been carried away from Jerusalem with the captives that had been carried away with Jeconiah king of Judah, whom Nebuchadnezzar the king of Babylon had carried away.

As summarized in the introduction, Nebuchadnezzar ruled over a great empire, but after a failed attempt to conquer Egypt, many of his vassal kings attempted to revolt. Rumblings from Judah caused him to invade in 597 BCE (or 432 BCE according to *Seder Olam*) to put down the revolution and install a new king. He gathered thousands of the leaders of the land, including its king and prophets and exiled them to Babylonia. It is from this group that Mordecai or Kish is to have come. Eleven years later, a further revolt caused Nebuchadnezzar to return and destroy the city of Jerusalem, including Solomon's Temple.

7 And he brought up Hadassah, that is, Esther, his uncle's daughter; for she had neither father nor mother, and the maiden was beautiful and fair to look on; and with the deaths of her father and mother, Mordecai took her for his own daughter.

According to the conventional timeline and the language of this book, Mordecai would have been carried away with the then king of Judah, Jeconiah/Jehoiachin in 597 BCE. And, if as many classical historians believed, Achashverosh was, in fact Xerxes, then Mordecai became prime minister well over 100 years later. Logic and recorded history now weigh heavily against the conclusion that the book takes place in the time of Xerxes (see comments on Chapter 1:1). And, linguistically, Artaxerxes is a better match for Achashverosh as the king of that time.

The early Jewish sages merge all of these into the king known to the Bible as Achashverosh and to the Greeks as Artaxerxes II in their Greek language version of the Megillah. Since the seemingly verifiable historic events described in Esther could not have happened under the rule of the king they know as Xerxes, the events of Esther must have taken place even later.

On the other hand, according to the timeline of the Jewish sages, it was only about 55 years after the destruction of the Temple by Nebuchadnezzar that Mordecai was living in Shushan/Susa.

In either case, it is reasonable to accept that Mordecai lived first in Babylon and tha⁻ he was from the tribe of Benjamin. It is just a matter of when he arrived in Shushan/Susa. Like ibn Ezra, we can assume that his line goes back to Kish and King Saul. The fact that both he and Esther seem to have migrated to Susa from Babylon is typical of behavior described in Persian treasury tablets that show free men of all ethnicities from across the empire routinely migrating to Susa to live and work.

Both the conventional and biblical dating assumes that the Mordecai of our story was born in Babylonia. Historians note that his name contained that of the Babylonian god, Marduk. Names that included pagcn deities were known to reflect the beliefs of the family of the bearer. This also applies to Esther whose name may be synonymous with Ishtar, a Babylonian goddess. And Haddassah could be the Babylonian Hutossa or Greek, Atossa. Or we may simply be told of the second name, Haddassah, because that was her Jewish name. Perhaps, Esther came from a somewhat more traditionally Jewish background than did Mordecai, but under his upbringing became disconnected from that legacy.

Divine providence 's implied in much of the text of the story. The Babylonian Talmud discusses the Hebrew meaning of the name Esther (hidden) in tractate Chullin, page 139b: "Where is there a hint to Esther in the Torah? 'Va-anokhi haster astir', I shall surely hide (my face . . .)."

8 So it came to pass, when the king's commandment and his decree was published, and when many maidens were gathered together to Shushan the castle, to the custody of Hegai, that Esther was taken into the king's house, to the custody of Hegai, keeper of the women.

9 And the maiden pleased him, and she obtained his kindness; and he speedily gave her ointments, with her portions, and the seven maidens, who were assigned to be given her out of the king's house; and he changed her position and that of her maidens for the better in the house of the women.

Like all ancient kings, Achashverosh was attended by eunuchs, some of whom must certainly have been Jewish and sympathetic to Mordecai and the plight of their people (see Ezra/Nechemia and Daniel for references to Jewish eunuchs). Persian and Greek kings only trusted eunuchs in their courts and imported them from the many provinces of their far-flung empires. Hegai was certainly a eunuch and may have been a Jew, and therefore favorably disposed toward Esther.

10 Esther had not made known her people nor her origin; for Mordecai had commanded her that she should not tell.

By this point in the story it is known that Haman is already the king's favorite minister. He was soon to become the Prime Minister. As a result of the circumstances described below, he had approved of a campaign of persecution toward the Jews.

Haman would owe his rise to power to originating and implementing a plan that involved the religious consolidation of the empire.

Heinrich Graetz, 19th century Polish author of the *History of the Jews*, and colleague and friend of the pillar of German orthodoxy, Samson Rafael Hirsch, describes a progression of religious persecution against the Jews in Persia, commencing well before the selection of Esther as queen. Graetz assumes that as Jews were persecuted and martyred, many secularized Jews woke up to their faith and protested the ill treatment of their brothers.

11 And every day Mordecai walked before the court of the women's house, to know the status of Esther, and what would become of her.

As perhaps the only Jew within the palace walls, in Shushan HaBira, he had unique access to Esther and the harem.

12 Now when the turn of every maiden came to go in to king Achashverosh, after it had been done to her according to the law for the women, twelve months--for so were the days of their anointing accomplished, six months with oil of myrrh, and six month with sweet odors, and with other ointments of the women—

The ancient "anointing" process was not a religious activity, but a cleansing activity.

Women in the ancient royal harem came from all corners of the kingdom, and many of their ethnic homelands and domestic circumstances were comparatively "uncivilized." The cleansing process was both sanitary and sociological. In order to keep company with the king, personal preparations also had to be made to elevate one's social status. After a sustained cleansing effort, attention was given to enhancing both appearance and aroma.

Monotheistic religions had both previously and subsequently associated the idea of anointing one's body with a cleansing of the spirit. While this does not appear to have been part of the ritual described here, Zoroastrians did have such practices.

13 when then the maiden came to the king, whatever she asked was given to go with her out of the house of the women to the king's house.

14 In the evening she went, and in the morning she returned to the second house of the women, to the custody of Shaashgaz, the king's chamberlain, who kept the concubines; she came in unto the king no more, except if the king delighted in her, and she was called by name.

There were two houses for the women, one for the virgins and another for the concubines.

15 Now when it was the turn of Esther, the daughter of Avichail the uncle of Mordecai, who had taken her for his daughter, to go in to the king, she required nothing but what Hegai the king's chamberlain, the keeper of the women, appointed. And Esther obtained favor in the eyes of all that looked upon her.

16 So Esther was taken to king Achashverosh into his royal house in the tenth month, which is the month Teveth, in the seventh year of his reign.

Four years had elapsed since the coronation party that led to the ouster of Vashti as queen. Esther had probably lived in the harem for a period of years in anticipation of meeting the king for the first time. And the king had likely met most of the other women in the harem before meeting Esther.

The names of the months used here in the Megillah are the same as those used today. These were adopted in Babylonia and retained thereafter, in whatever kingdom the Jews dwelled.

17 And the king loved Esther more than all the women, and she obtained greater grace and kindness in his sight than all the virgins; so that he set the royal crown upon her head, and made her queen in place of Vashti.

Esther had won the competition. She became the favorite both within the harem with Hegai, its supervisor, and now with the king himself. She was given the title of queen, which until now had been vacant.

It appears to have taken a period of years for the king to literally "measure" each of the candidates from his harem for the post of queen. That he first encounters Esther after having experienced many other candidates is providential, or at least fortuitous.

18 Then the king made a great feast for all his princes and his servants-- Esther's feast; and he made a release to the provinces, and gave gifts, according to the generosity of the king.

19 And the virgins were gathered together the second time. Meanwhile, Mordecai sat in the king's gate.

This second gathering seems to be mentioned by the author as if it is significant in fixing a time for the plot which Mordecai is soon to uncover.

The second gathering of the women is also no longer a gathering of virgins. Those who have been with the king will now go to the second house, that of the concubines (per Bertheau). Or, some believe that a second gathering of the remaining virgins may have been used to further support the elevated status of Esther who was now identified as queen.

Still others believe that mentioning the gathering was simply a vehicle to emphasize that even the selection of a queen would not retard the king's polygamous ways (Cornelius A. Lapide, 16th century priest and Biblical commentator).

20 Esther had not told of her origin or her people as Mordecai had commanded her; for Esther followed the instructions of Mordecai, just as when she was brought up with him.

At this point in the story, at least seven years into the reign of Achashverosh (Artaxerxes II cs proposed here), construction of the Temple had been halted and persecution of the Jews was ongoing. Changes had been made to Zoroastrian worship and while these changes had been generally accepted around the empire, Jews were notable for their resistance. Hiding her religious identity was instrumental to Esther's acceptance in the harem and ultimately to her royal entrée.

21 in those days, while Mordecai sat in the king's gate, two of the king's chamberlains, Bigthan and Teresh, among those that kept the door, were angry, and sought to lay hands on the king Achashverosh.

Bigthan and Teresh were among the cadre of guards at the gate of the palace, and were angry with the king.

They wanted to "lay hand" on the king, the same phrase used in Chapter 3, verse 6 below when Haman wants to do away with Mordecai.

The word for "anger" (קָצַף) used here is the same as that of the Book of Exodus to describe Pharaoh's angry imprisonment of his cupbearer and baker. The active parallels are significant: In Mordecai's case this becomes his opportunity to be honored by the king and ultimately to overcome Haman. In Joseph's case he is spurred to ask for his freedom and is ultimately honored by the king. In both cases there are two men who offend the king. In both cases the "sin" is a conspiracy against the crown. And in both cases the good deeds of our principals go unrewarded for some time.

There are a number of other parallels between the *Book of Esther* and the story of Joseph in the *Book of Genesis*.

Joseph's father Jacob says, "v'cha'asher shacholti shacholti," (Genesis 43:14, "if events do not go well, and I will be bereaved, then I will be bereaved") while Esther says "v'cha'asher avoditi avoditi."(Esther 4:16, if events do not go well, and I perish, then I will perish.") The words, "megillat Esther" mean both the megillah/story of Esther and "to reveal that which is hidden." The name given to Joseph by the Egyptian pharaoh is Tzofnat Pa'aneach which has the same meaning. Both Esther and Joseph are referred to as "yefat toar vifat mareh (beautiful in appearance)." And both Mordecai and Joseph rise suddenly to prominence in the Diaspora, each becoming second in command to an all- powerful king. Both are descendants of the matriarch, Rachel.

In other words, while the language and content of the Megillah do not appear to be overtly religious, the form and style of the story were shaped by an author quite familiar with references and allusions to well-known Biblical texts.

22 And the thing became known to Mordecai, who told it to Esther the queen; and Esther told it to the king in Mordecai's name.

Sitting at the gate of the city, Mordecai was likely able to overhear their plans. While some commentators attribute this to Mordecai's ability to understand many languages (as legend has it so could all the members of the Anshei Knesset Hag'dolah), it is even more likely that Mordecai was conversant in the local languages of commerce and society in which he was involved on a daily basis.

23 And when the matter was looked into and it was found to be so, they were both hanged on a tree; and it was written in the book of the chronicles before the king.

Esther Chapter 3

1 After these things king Achashverosh did promote Haman the son of Hammedatha the Agagite, and advanced him, and set his seat above all the princes that were with him.

The Megillah's Hamon was the son of Hammedatha, in the conventional chronology the name of a Magian usurper of the Persian throne (also called Smerdis). His roots were probably in the Magian (a mystical, polytheistic faith) priesthood.

There may have been a genealogical link connecting Haman to Agag/Amalek. But this may also have been a later addition to the text, or a purposeful embellishment by an author steeped in the Biblical narrative and its implications.

Most historians believe that Haman could not have been a descendent of Agag. Amalek was destroyed by Saul and Agag was killed by Samuel (1 Samuel 25). The other tribes of Amalek were destroyed in the time of Hezekiah (1 Chronicles 4:43), so to have been known as an Agagite seems unusual. The Greek version of Esther follows this line as it does not include any reference to Agag/Amalek.

Yet this addition draws a powerful religious parallel between the earlier biblical battle of Amalek and Israel with that of the tribe of Benjamin (here represented by Mordecai) and Amalek (here represented by Haman) in ancient Persia.

Just as the author uses the stylistic similarities of the stories of Joseph and Mordecai to build a spiritual context, the conflict between Amalek and Israe is used to impress upon the reader that this battle is not limited to ancient Persia but is eternal and will torment the Jews until the end of days.

2 And all the king's servants, that were in the king's gate, bowed down, and prostrated themselves to Haman; for the king had so commanded concerning him. But Mordecai did not bow, nor prostrate himself.

Biblical commentators explain that Mordecai was demonstrably rejecting idol worship. Haman was demanding fealty to his idols and to his embodiment of them, and Mordecai publically rejected this demand.

The *Book of Esther* opens with Persian monotheism under attack. Greek historians record that the consolidation of the Persian kingdom under Artaxerxes II was threatened by the conflict between state monotheism and its disparate polytheistic faiths. As a result, a plan was created to combine polytheistic religious practices with the state religion of Zoroaster. The *Book of Esther* presents a candidate for authorship of that strategy (Haman) who was then appointed the king's prime minister and given unfettered power to implement his plan.

The early rulers of the Medo-Persian empire were Achaemenian (a dynasty initiated by conqueror and king Achaemenes), and credited their success to the one God, Ahura Mazda. Zoroastrianism was not only a monotheistic faith but it rejected all forms of image worship. "In the Persian period, the Jews encountered a religion that was different in many respects from the religions that they had known hitherto, a religion that did not recognize idols." (Ephraim Urbach, writing in his, *The Sages*, p.20)

After the Achaemenian conquest of the Babylonian empire, the pressure of religious assimilation must have dramatically eased for the already largely secularized Jewish community. While Jews may not have observed Jewish halachik, separatist practices, they were uncomfortable with avodah zara/idol worship. The difference between Ahura Mazda and the God of the Jews must have been indistinguishable to the Persians. Religious or not, while in Babylonia Jews were distinctive because they rejected idols -- in Persia they lost this distinction under the umbrella of Zoroastrianism.

Based on the antiquity of the language of the Gathas and Avesta (holy writings of Zoroastrianism in a predecessor tongue to Sanskrit) the prophet Zoroaster (also known as Zarathustra) probably lived a century or two after the Jews left Egypt. Primary to Zoroastrian thought are the ideas of truth and "active" free will, all bound up in fealty to the one God, Ahura Mazda. Historians routinely assume that Judaism borrowed these ideas from Zoroastrianism, but as can be demonstrated, the Torah predates this Middle Eastern, monotheistic faith.

Greek historians later equated the faith of Zoroaster with magic and polytheism, though this is far from its monotheistic roots. Medieval Christians even equated Zoroaster with the Biblical Nimrod and the invention of astrology. So it is clear that much about true Zoroastrianism was and remains unknown, but that contemporary practice and philosophy is dramatically different from the original, as practiced at the time of Mordecai and Esther.

According to the conventional timeline, when Darius II took the throne he demonstrated his monotheistic zeal by allowing the Jews to return to Jerusalem and begin rebuilding the Temple. As mentioned above, after his death, his successor, Artaxerxes/Achashverosh was determined to inject Babylonian polytheism into the state religion to help consolidate the far-flung empire. His advisors actively influenced him in this matter.

According to the later Babylonian priest and historian Berosus and from cuneiform tablets, there were no images of gods in Persia until the reign of Artaxerxes II. He brought back belief in Anahita and Mithra, old Babylonian gods that had been abandoned by true Zoroastrians. When these idols and their temples were introduced, the religious Jews in the kingdom must have suddenly become visible and noteworthy for their disloyalty. Graetz confirms this progression in his *History of the Jews* as well and notes that persecution of the Jews followed.

Since the Zoroastrian clergy seemed to have accepted the introduction of idols and pagan gods, Haman, the king's prime minister, must have been quite surprised to find a distinct ethnic group within Persia that resisted the new paganism.

And it is very likely that the Persians had not previously come across the Jews at all. Josephus quotes Herodotus as stating that "the Phoenicians and Syrians in Palestine (who are assumed by Josephus to connote Jews) owed their receiving circumcision from the Egyptians." Herodotus, who lived during and wrote about the early Persian period never names the Jews in his works.

It is during the Persian period, after the destruction of the First Temple in Jerusalem, and after the Jewish resettlement in Babylonia that the perception of the Jews began to change. It was ". . . under the Persians that *Jew* changed from a primarily sociopolitical term to a primarily religious one." (Mark Hamilton, *Jewish Ethnicity During the Achaemenid Period*, writing in the Restoration Quarterly, 1995)

3 Then the king's servants,that were in the king's gate, said to Mordecai: 'Why do you transgress the king's commandment?'

4 Now it came to pass, when they spoke to him day after day, and he did not heed them, that they told Haman, to see if Mordecai's words would stand; because he had told them that he was a Jew.

The language here recalls Genesis 39:10: "When she spoke to Joseph day after day and he did not heed her." In that case, the wife of Potiphar the Egyptian unsuccessfully attempted to seduce Joseph time and time again. Neither Mordecai nor Joseph would succumb to the orders of an authoritative pagan at the expense of their innate moral and ideological beliefs.

5 And when Haman saw that Mordecai did not bow down, nor prostrate himself before him, then was Haman full of wrath.

6 and it seemed contemptible in his eyes to lay hands on Mordecai alone; for they had told him of the people of Mordecai; Haman sought to destroy all the Jews that were throughout the whole kingdom of Achashverosh, the people of Mordecai.

Just as Haman convinced Achashverosh that it was necessary to apply his anger with Vashti to all women of the empire, so too did he seek to punish not just Mordecai, but all of his people.

In a broader religious context, Mordecai's reaction to Haman's innovations in Zoroastrianism made it clear to Haman that there was going to be a more significant problem than just the recalcitrance of a single Jew. To force universal compliance, Haman needed to erase the Jewish religion, not necessarily the Jews themselves. And for that reason he promulgated his decree almost a year before it was to be carried out. He was careful to give the Jews time to reconsider their behavior (see verse 14 below).

But, since the Jews seemed not to be cowed by individual persecutions and punishments, they would have to be addressed as a group for his plan to succeed.

The conflict between Haman and Mordecai was symbolic of the existential struggle between polytheism and monotheism at this time (i.e. the casting of lots to see what the gods would have happen and when).

Elephantine papyri (Cowley 22 and others) indicate that the Jews under Persian rule in Egypt had friction with their gentile neighbors there as well. The Egyptians had a long-standing hatred of the Jews, heightened at that time by the behavior of the Persian monarchy – behavior that protected the temple constructed by the Jews in Elephantine (an important Persian, military outpost under the protection of both Jews and other ethnicities under Persian rule). Early Persian policy supported religious unity in each of the ethnic groups of its empire. Despite this, the Persian commander in Elephantine conspired with his Egyptian troops to destroy the Jewish temple there.

7 In the first month, which is the month Nisan, in the twelfth year of king Achahverosh, they cast pur/lot before Haman from day to day, and from month to month, to the twelfth month, which is the month Adar.

The casting of lots was customary at this time of year, the New Year in Babylonian times. Nisan was the first month of the year, and a 10 day festival at the temple of Marduk included the drawing of lots to determine the nature of the upcoming year.

In fact, the Jewish New Year ritual in Temple times involved a similar act on the part of the Kohain Gadol (high priest) who would cast lots to choose between two goats to help expiate the sins of the people and determine tidings for the year ahead.

8 And Haman said to king Achashverosh: 'There is a certain people scattered and dispersed among the peoples in all the provinces of thy kingdom; and their laws differ from those of all other people; and they do not keep the king's laws; therefore it does not benefit the king to leave them alone.

In contrast to the Biblical praise given the Jews for being a people "who dwells apart and is not counted among the nations." (Numbers, Chapter 23, verse 9), Haman denigrated their differences. But the Jews of Persia did live among the other nations of the empire and had both social and mercantile intercourse with them. As a result, the festival of Purim (established later in the text) was not ordered by the Jewish, religious elite, but by Mordecai and Esther who were comfortable in Persian society and steeped in its customs.

As commented upon above, their given names were those of assimilated Babylonians, and contained the names of local gods. Mordecai permitted Esther to marry a non-Jew (common in Ezra's time – the family of the Kohen Gadol was related to the Samaritan ruler Sanballat, for example).

Mordecai chose to make an issue of image worship after months or perhaps years of religious persecution by Artaxerxes/Achashverosh. His defiance of Haman highlights the fact that Jews at all levels of observance were unwilling to go against certain fundamental tenants of traditional Jewish faith.

When the Jews resisted these new religious rites, severe measures had to be implemented in order to keep their resistance from spreading to their neighbors, the strict Zoroastrians. For this reason, Haman brought the issue to the king's attention.

9 If it please the king, let it be written that they be destroyed; and I will pay ten thousand talents of silver into the hands of those in charge of the king's business, to bring it into the king's treasuries.

Haman's offer of 10,000 talents of silver is quantitatively consistent with a report by Herodotus (*Histories*, 3:95) on the cost of Xerxes' earlier failed campaign against the Greeks.

Firmly engaged in commerce since their Babylonian days, the Jews had accumulated significant social standing and wealth. That wealth would go to the king's treasury to compensate for the loss of Haman's royal allocation to the cause.

The value of 10,000 talents was estimated by Jacob Hoschander (early twentieth century historian and teacher at the Jewish Theological Seminary) as $18 million in 1920 dollars, based on a recorded calculation of the cost of Xerxes' earlier failed campaign against Greece. So Haman offered both the king and Persian citizens a deal whose economics were compelling.

10 And the king took his ring from his hand, and gave it to Haman the son of Hammedatha the Agagite, enemy of the Jews.

Haman is not associated with Agag/Amalek in the later Greek version of Esther. Here Haman is the enemy of the Jews for two reasons: first, because of their refusal to accede to the religious changes instituted 'n the empire, and second because of the Biblical animus of Amalek to the Jews.

All of this happens, of course, without the king ever asking just who this obnoxious people might be. And it is quite possible that their being described as dispersed throughout the land offered no real hint, since during the Assyrian conquests which preceded those of the Babylonians and Persians, ethnic groups were routinely mixed together to dilute their ethnic, communal identity and strength and, consequently, their potential as a threat to the empire.

11 And the king said to Haman: 'The silver is given to thee, the people also, to do with them as it seems good in your eyes.'

The transfer of wealth is a bribe for the non-Jews who would otherwise have had no reason to acquiesce in the extermination of their neighbors the Jews. Esther later emphasizes this when she says that "we have been sold . . ." in chapter 7, verse 4.

12 Then were the king's scribes called in the first month, on the thirteenth day, and there was written, according to all that Haman commanded to the king's satraps and to the governors that were over every province, and to the princes of every people; to every province according to the writing thereof, and to every people after their language; in the name of king Achashverosh was it written, and it was sealed with the king's ring.

The author makes the case that the decree was of the sort that was not reversible, i.e., one that was royally sealed.

13 And letters were sent by runners into all the king's provinces, to destroy, to slay, and to wipe out, all Jews, both young and old, little children and women, in one day, the thirteenth day of the twelfth month, which is the month Adar, and to take the spoil of them for a prey.

History records that it might take up to three months for a horseman to deliver a message from one end of the kingdom to the other. Yet, Haman allows an entire year – hoping that the Jews will accept the prescribed religious practices as had Zoroastrians. Should the Jews capitulate, Haman would achieve his goal without disturbance or cost. Should their obstinacy prevail, the royal coffers would be reimbursed several times over.

The edict also encouraged Persian citizens to seize the belongings of the Jews. Contrast this with the moral code of the Jews, depicted in chapter 9, verses 10, 15 and 16, which prohibits them from taking spoil from the vanquished.

14 The copy of the writing, to be given out for a decree in every province, was to be publicized to all people, that they should be ready for that day.

The Persian empire included dozens of ethnicities and languages. For the decree to be effective it had to be published in every language of the empire.

15 The messengers went forth in haste by the king's commandment, and the decree was given out in Shushan the castle; and the king and Haman sat down to drink; but the city of Shushan was perplexed.

While the decree had effected little drama in Shushan HaBira (the palace), it created pandemonium in the city outside. In the home of the greatest concentration of Jews in the empire,

Jews were at a loss to find any solace in what appeared to them to be a death sentence.

Herodotus notes that Persian monarchs deliberated on important decisions when they were drunk and would have their chief advisors present, just as is the case here. Later Esther takes advantage of this custom when she asks the "king and Haman to come to the banquet I have prepared for him." Some conventional historians see this request of Esther's as betraying the book as literary fiction. yet, as seen here, it is completely consistent with royal custom.

As recorded by Ctesias, before being murdered by Artaxerxes, Cyrus wrote what Esther subsequently learned -- that Cyrus was the better philosopher of the two kings and that he could both drink more wine and hold it better than Artaxerxes/Achashverosh.

Esther Chapter 4

1 And Mordecai knew all that had happened, and Mordecai rent his clothes, and put on sackcloth with ashes, and he went out into the midst of the city, and cried a loud and a bitter cry;

Mordecai had earlier defied Haman and revealed himself as a Jew. Yet he had cautioned Esther to keep her status secret, even though his relationship to Esther was not.

2 and he even came before the king's gate; for none might enter the king's gate clothed in sackcloth.

But now he seems to throw caution to the wind, daring those who might be close to the king to see his display of mourning. He is most interested, of course, in attracting the attention of Esther.

3 And in every province, wherever the king's commandment and his decree came, there was great mourning among the Jews, and fasting, and weeping, and wailing; and many lay in sackcloth and ashes.

Mordecai has set the trend through his public mourning – first in the city itself, and then in front of the king's palace in Shushan HaBira.

4 And Esther's maidens and her chamberlains came and told her; and the queen was distraught; and she sent clothing to dress Mordecai; and to take his sackcloth from off him; but he did not accept it.

Our protagonist is called Mordecai the Jew, even before the king was likely to have discovered that fact. Mordecai had already made a public display of his defiance of Haman, so many obviously knew of his Jewishness. Yet, Esther now sends Mordecai new clothes so as to conceal this fact from the king even as Mordecai sits in torn clothes at the king's gate, mourning over the proclamation against the Jews.

5 Then Esther called for Hathach, one of the king's chamberlains, whom he had appointed to attend upon her, and charged him to go to Mordecai, to know what this was, and why it was.

While it is unlikely that Esther did not know of the decree against the Jews (since Mordecai himself was able to pass along messages through sympathetic members of the royal staff), her reaction is testimony to just how insulated the royal family and harem were from the operations and activities of the empire. She needed to solicit news that was evident to those outside the palace. This may be a comment as well on just how far Esther had removed herself from her people.

6 So Hathach went forth to Mordecai to the main street of the city, which was before the king's gate.

Mordecai had located himself at the gate of the city, immediately outside of the king's palace in order to exert pressure on Esther to assume a role in saving her people. Mordecai's presence outside the palace in the garb of a mourner could not be ignored.

7 And Mordecai told him of all that had happened to him, and the exact sum of the money that Haman had promised to pay to the king's treasuries for the Jews, to destroy them.

Haman fully expected that he would profit from the destruction of the Jews. The wealth that they had accumulated would revert to the state treasury, increasing both the king's coffers and his own.

At the same time, Mordecai chose to specify the enormous sum that Haman offered to pay to "buy" the Jews, no doubt to stoke Esther's ire against Haman.

8 And he gave him the copy of the writing of the decree that was given out in Shushan to destroy them, to show it to Esther, and to read it to her; and to command her to go in to the king, to supplicate him, and to solicit him on behalf of her people.

There was no reason for the decree to have been distributed earlier in Shushan HaBira, because no Jews lived there.

9 And Hathach came and told Esther the words of Mordecai.

10 Then Esther spoke to Hathach, and gave him a message for Mordecai:

11 'All the king's servants, and the people of the king's provinces, do know, that any man or woman who will come to the king to the inner court, who is not called, there is one law for him, that he be put to death, except to whom the king shall hold out the

golden sceptre, that he may live; but I have not been called to come in to the king now for thirty days.'

Esther's response pointedly ignores her attachment to the Jews as well as her status as "Queen" among the women of the harem (Hathach has been appointed by the king to attend to her alone). She presents herself as just an ordinary member of the harem.

12 And they told to Mordecai Esther's words.

At this point it is not just Hathach who is the go between, but a group of attendants. If Hathach was a Jew as is supposed by many commentators, he may have recruited others to try to rally Esther to the cause of the Jews.

13 Then Mordecai asked them to return/respond to Esther: 'Think not that thou shalt escape in the king's house, more than all the Jews.

Mordecai had succeeded in getting Esther's attention. His plan was to force her to see that her own survival was going to be at risk either at the hand of the king, should he so desire, or as a result of the decree instigated by Haman. Her only chance for survival was to risk soliciting the king.

He now sends her a message, not only in the hand of Hathach but in the hands of many, that delivers the ultimate message of Jewish survival and faith. This message inspires both the messengers and Esther to act:

14 For if thou altogether hold thy peace at this time, then will relief and deliverance arise to the Jews from another place, but thou and thy father's house will perish; and who knows whether you have not come to royalty for such a time as this?'

Even though Mordecai and Esther were comfortably assimilated formerly in Babylonian and now Persian society, they still held the traditional perspective that the Jews would be providentially saved from calamity. By reminding Esther that salvation would come in one form or another at some point, Mordecai encouraged her to believe that if she was destined to be the tool of that salvation her efforts would be successful.

Correspondence uncovered in Elephantine, Egypt, dating from this era demonstrates both the Jewish dedication to the God of Israel and an ambivalence toward and occasional embrace of polytheism. While letters from Elephantine to Judea do not mention a Jewish embrace of pagan gods, the Cowley papyri reveal a fascinating fact: The Jews of Elephantine collected funds to support the temple that they had constructed there. However, the dispersal of those funds was shared with Eshembethel and Anathbethel, two manifestations of the Aramean god, Bethel.

15 Then Esther told them to return and answer Mordecai:

16 'Go, gather all the Jews that are in Shushan, and fast for me, and neither eat nor drink three days, night or day; I and my maidens will also fast in like manner; and so will I go in unto the king, which is not according to the law; and if I perish, I perish.'

Maimonides writes that the Fast of Esther that we observe today on the day before Purim commemorates Esther's three day fast. He also states that we observe it in the month of Adar today rather than in Nissan (when the decree was issued) because we do not commemorate mourning during the month of Nissan.

The Midrash Tanchuma and Tractate Sophrim of the Babylonian Talmud both refer to this one-day fast as do texts written shortly after the Talmudic period. The Megillat Taanit, which lists the various fast days observed by the Jewish people, does not list this fast, so it seems to have been added in or after the Talmudic period in order to enhance the serious nature of the holiday.

"Of what then is the Fast of Esther a warning? Of the error of buying the favor of nations by adaptation to their way of life to the extent of violating Divinely imposed obligations. . . the Fast of Esther . . . proclaims to all generations of Israel: If God again tries them by means of the benevolence of nations as He did by the latter's cruelty, they must remain steadfast in this trial and meet the conciliatory kindnesses with loyalty and attachment and by furthering the welfare of the nations and by the full development of the beautiful character of Israel, as, indeed is demanded by God amid the harshness of nations – but not by the surrendering of Israel's spiritual self. For that would mean committing suicide in order to gain life." (*Horeb*, Samson Rafael Hirsch, Section 238)

Beginning shortly after the victory of the Maccabees over the Greeks, the holiday of Nicanor, celebrating the victory of Judah Maccabee over this Greek general, was added to the calendar. As recorded in *II Maccabees*, Nicanor Day was celebrated on the 14th of Adar, the day before Mordecai Day (Purim). This meant that the Fast of Esther in Talmudic times had to be moved to the day after Purim. However, there is no trace of the continued observance of Nicanor Day after the 7th century, which allowed the fast to resume its place preceding Purim since that time.

17 So Mordecai went his way, and did according to all that Esther had commanded him.

Mordecai was in no position to either negotiate or further strategize. Esther was about to put her life in jeopardy. The burden of success was squarely on her shoulders. By assuming this risk, her instructions took on the character of "commands."

Esther Chapter 5

1 Now it came to pass on the third day, that Esther put on her royal apparel, and stood in the inner court of the king's house, very close to the king's house; and the king sat upon his royal throne in the royal house, very close to the entrance of the house.

She deliberately put herself in full view of the king, intentionally avoiding interception by one of his attendants. In Chapter 6:5 Haman wants to see the king but must be announced by an attendant.

2 And when the king saw Esther the queen standing in the court, she obtained favor in his eyes; and the king held out to Esther the golden sceptre that was in his hand. And Esther drew near, and touched the top of the sceptre.

In resisting the entreaties of Mordecai to engage the king for the benefit of her people, Esther alluded to her having fallen out of favor with the king because she had not been called by him for over a month. In a typical Persian harem, that period was often a year. Again, Esther was not like the others in the harem. She was his public favorite, as was seen in chapter 2, verses 17 and 18.

3 Then the king said to her: 'What wilt thou, Esther the queen? for whatever thy request, even to half of the kingdom, it shall be given to thee.'

4 And Esther said: 'If it seem good to the king, let the king and Haman come this day to the banquet that I have prepared for him.'

Again, there is an allusion to the comment of Herodotus that Persian monarchs deliberated on important decisions only under the influence of wine and with their chief advisors present. Appropriately, Esther asked the king to come together with Haman to the *banquet of wine* (verse 6 below). Esther knew that this would both make the king more comfortable and raise Haman's expectations.

5 Then the king said: 'Cause Haman to hurry to do as Esther hath said.' So the king and Haman came to the banquet that Esther had prepared.

One action follows closely on another as Esther allows no time for Haman to discover her real motive. The text describes a rapid turn of events, much like those surrounding Joseph who was elevated from slave to royalty overnight.

6 And the king said to Esther at the banquet of wine: 'Whatever thy petition, it shall be granted; and whatever thy request, even to half of the kingdom, it shall be performed.'

In verse 3 the king supplicates Esther, offering her half of his kingdom. But she requests no "thing." Instead, she asks for the king's blind participation in her plan. Now the king again tries to satisfy her desires, assuming that she will once more request nothing material, but only his action (וְתֵעָשׂ) which he is more than willing to provide.

7 Then answered Esther, and said: 'My petition and my request is

8 if I have found favor in the eyes of the king, and if it please the king to grant my petition, and to perform my request--let the king and Haman come to the banquet that I shall prepare for them, and I will do tomorrow as the king hath said.'

9 Then Haman went out that day joyful and glad of heart; but when Haman saw Mordecai in the king's gate, and he did not stand, or move for him, Haman was filled with anger against Mordecai.

Was there reason for Mordecai to have remained at the king's gate? After all, Esther had set a plan in motion just as Mordecai had urged. Was it simply a matter of Mordecai "rubbing it in?"

On the contrary, Mordecai needed to generate sympathy in the royal residence. It was important that as many of the king's staff know of Mordecai's Jewishness as possible so that his earlier good deed in saving the king's life now be associated with not only a loyal servant, but a Jew – one threatened now with extinction.

10 Nevertheless Haman restrained himself, and went home; and he sent for and brought his friends and Zeresh his wife.

The introduction of Zeresh here is significant. Later she will testify to the providential nature of the relationship between the Jews and the Divine. Her advice is accepted without question by her husband, in this case concerning the erecting of a gallows on which to hang Mordecai (verse 14 below), and her later comments will be accepted similarly, albeit with very different implications.

11 And Haman recounted to them the glory of his riches, and the multitude/greatness of his sons, and everything as to how the king had promoted him, and how he had advanced him above the princes and servants of the king.

The sons of Haman were likely to have been well known and of standing in the Persian government, hence the mention of them here and individually by name later. When we read וְרֹב בָּנָיו it very well may mean the large number of sons that he had. But then, that would be nothing new to either his wife or friends.

Instead, he may have been bragging to his wife and friends that as his own stature had grown in the kingdom, so too had that of his sons (for a like meaning, see the use of "rov" in Exodus 14 for example). And he may have been telling this to his wife to surprise her with the good news, which he elaborates upon in the following verse.

12 Haman said moreover: ' Esther the queen did let no man come in with the king to the banquet that she had prepared but myself; and tomorrow also am I invited by her along with the king.

13 Yet all this availeth me nothing, so long as I see Mordecai the Jew sitting at the king's gate.'

14 *Then Zeresh his wife and all his friends said to him: 'Let a gallows be made fifty cubits high, and in the morning speak to the king that Mordecai may be hanged thereon; then go in merrily with the king to the banquet.' And the thing pleased Haman; and he caused the gallows to be made.*

Esther Chapter 6

1 *On that night the king could not sleep; and he commanded the book of records of the chronicles be brought, and they were read before the king.*

What would Esther request of the king at the banquet the next day? Perhaps a search of his personal records would hint at a solution to that mystery.

Though the language of the Megillah points to the king's fitful sleep as part of the providential plan, providence was at least partly dependent on the actions of Mordecai. Mordecai had by now made his constant presence at the king's gate known to all in Shushan HaBirah (Chapter 5:9). Had the king been advised of this he may have called for his book of records in order to refresh his memory concerning Mordecai's earlier act of loyalty.

Greek historians note that Persian kings routinely maintained personal chronicles. While they are referenced by ancient historians, they are no longer extant. These must have been lost or destroyed during the conquest of Persia by Alexander the Great whose fury spared no antiquity, no matter its value. Nevertheless, the Megillah refers to chronicles because at the time of its composition, such chronicles were available and could be consulted by the reader for historical and social context.

2 *And it was found written, that Mordecai had told of Bigthana and Teresh, two of the king's chamberlains, of those that kept the door, who had sought to lay hands on the king Achashverosh.*

See comments on Chapter 2:22.

3 And the king said: 'What honor and dignity hath been done to Mordecai for this?' Then said the king's servants that ministered unto him: 'Not a thing was done for him.'

As the Prime Minister, Haman would have been responsible for rewarding Mordecai. In the eyes of the king Haman was left wanting due to this failure.

4 And the king said: 'Who is in the court?'--Now Haman had come into the outer court of the king's house, to speak to the king to hang Mordecai on the gallows that he had prepared for him.

5 And the king's servants said to him: 'Behold, Haman stands in the court.' And the king said: 'Let him come in.'

6 And Haman came in. And the king said to him: 'What shall be done to the man whom the king delighteth to honor?'--Now Haman said in his heart: 'Whom would the king delight to honor more than myself?'

7 And Haman said unto the king: 'For the man whom the king delighteth to honor,

8 let royal apparel be brought which has been worn by the king, and the horse that the king rides upon, and on whose head a royal crown is set;

Why would it be an honor to wear clothing once worn by the king himself? Haman's answer recalls a similar story, recorded by the Greek historian, Plutarch, concerning another minister to Artaxerxes II, Tiribazus, who reveled in the opportunity to wear a garment of the king. In this instance it is an honor Haman wished for himself but was compelled to bestow on Mordecai.

9 *and let the apparel and the horse be delivered to the hand of one of the king's most noble princes, that they may dress the man therewith whom the king delights to honor, and cause him to ride on horseback through the street of the city, and proclaim before him: Thus shall it be done to the man whom the king delights to honor.'*

10 *And the king said to Haman: 'Make haste, and take the apparel and the horse, as thou hast said, and do so to Mordecai the Jew, that sits at the king's gate; let nothing fail of all that thou hast spoken.'*

Calling Mordecai, "the Jew" at this point makes sense. Mordecai has sought to bring attention to himself (Chapter 6:1), to draw the attention of the king to his earlier loyal service. And that loyal service is rewarded, "despite" the fact that he is a Jew.

11 *And Haman took the apparel and the horse, and dressed Mordecai, and caused him to ride through the street of the city, and proclaimed before him: 'Thus shall be done unto the man whom the king delights to honor.'*

12 *And Mordecai returned to the king's gate. But Haman rushed to his house, mourning and covering his head.*

13 *And Haman recounted to Zeresh his wife and all his friends everything that had befallen him. Then said his wise men and Zeresh his wife to him: 'If Mordecai, before whom thou hast begun to fall, be of the seed of the Jews, thou shalt not overcome him, but shalt surely fall before him.'*

Zeresh warns her husband of his certain failure against the special providence of the Jews, even though they had been exiled from their homeland and scattered throughout the empire. As is the case with a number of other entries, this verse clearly enhances the religious tenor of the text.

14 They were yet talking with him, when the king's chamberlains arrived, and hastened to bring Haman to the banquet that Esther had prepared.

Esther Chapter 7

1 And the king and Haman came to banquet (to drink) with Esther the queen.

As the language here makes very clear, the very idea of a banquet connoted drinking and, in Esther's mind, a more easily influenced king. And, as alcohol was historically part of the royal decision-making process, any judgments rendered in that drunken state would, Esther knew, have the power of law and would be carried out without equivocation.

2 And the king said again to Esther on the second day at the banquet of wine: 'Whatever thy petition, queen Esther, it shall be granted thee; and whatever thy request, even to half of the kingdom, it shall be performed.'

This is the third time that Achashverosh asks Esther for her petition. He addresses her as Queen and he knows that the request will be for something more important than just another banquet.

In this verse and in verse 3 that follows, the verb וְתִנָּתֶן is feminine, while in verses 5:3 and 5:6 the verb is masculine. Unlike the earlier petitions, Esther's now making a very personal petition for her own life!

3 Then Esther the queen answered and said: 'If I have found favor in your eyes, O king, and if it please the king, let my life be given me at my petition, and my people at my request;

Esther addresses the king in the second person, not the third as is customarily the case. She is wagering that the intimacy of their relationship will save her people from annihilation, because, for the first time, Esther reveals that she too is a Jew.

4 for we are sold, I and my people, to be destroyed, to be killed, and to perish. But if we had been sold for slaves and concubines, I had held my peace, for the adversary is not worthy that the king be damaged.'

Esther remarks that her people have been sold (chapter 3, verse 11). And she bristles at the fact that an actual monetary transaction has been made in which she and her people are chattel.

The use of the word נִמְכַּרְנוּ here is not different from its use in Nechemia, chapter 5, verse 8 where he buys back the lives of Jews from the Gentiles. Esther implies that this affront to her and to her people is an affront to the throne. Esther is careful to assign blame for the impending attacks on Haman, an unworthy adversary to the throne, not on the king in whose name the edict was written and will be carried out.

5 Then spoke the king Achashverosh and said to Esther the queen: 'Who is he, and where is he, that filled his heart to do so?'

6 And Esther said: 'An adversary and an enemy, this is wicked Haman.' Then Haman was terrified before the king and the queen.

7 And the king arose in his wrath from the banquet of wine and went into the palace garden; but Haman stood to seek his life from Esther the queen; for he saw that there was evil determined against him by the king.

8 Then the king returned from the palace garden into the place of the banquet of wine; and Haman was fallen upon the couch whereon Esther was. Then said the king: 'Will he even force the

queen before me in the house?' As the word went out of the king's mouth, they covered Haman's face.

9 Then said Charbonah, one of the chamberlains that was before the king: 'Behold also, the gallows, which Haman made for Mordecai, who spoke good for the king, stands in the house of Haman fifty cubits high.' And the king said: 'Hang him thereon.'

According to Herodotus the king would not put one to death for a single fault. In chapter 6 verse 1 the king could not sleep and he requested his book of personal chronicles. That Mordecai's deed had gone unrewarded reflected poorly on Haman, the prime minister to whom the plot and its revelation were brought.

But in having Charbona reveal Haman plotting against Mordecai, a "second strike" s recorded that resulted in Haman's immediate condemnation. "Gam Charvonah zachor l'tov." For this, Charbona is remembered for good among the Jews forever.

10 And they hanged Haman on the gallows that he had prepared for Mordecai. And the king's wrath was assuaged.

Esther Chapter 8

1 On that day did the king Achashverosh give to Esther the queen the house of Haman the Jews' enemy. And Mordecai came before the king; for Esther had told what he was to her.

The fate of Haman is sealed on the gallows (Chapter 7:10). That the ten sons of Haman had the same fate befall them as their father is historically characteristic of the Persian rule of law.

Possessions of the condemned became property of the crown. And so the king could transfer that property to Esther, his queen. In addition, the state would visit the same punishment on the family of the condemned as befell him (references in both Herodotus and Plutarch). With the wealth of Haman and his sons now under her control, Esther was able to raise the status of Mordecai in the eyes of the people by placing the wealth of Haman in his hands.

During her candidacy for the harem, Esther's relationship to Mordecai must have become widely known in the city of Shushan. However, in the palace, it does not become known until this time.

2 And the king took off his ring, which he had taken from Haman, and gave it to Mordecai. And Esther set Mordecai over the house of Haman.

Notes to the first chapter of the book explained that the king of Persia at this time added to the size of his empire during his reign. "And the king Achashverosh laid a tribute upon the land, and upon the isles of the sea." (Esther 10:1)

Mordecai now replaces Haman as the Prime Minister and as such will negotiate the Peace of Antalcidas with Sparta, expanding the Persian Empire to the "isles of the sea." Both the timing and acquisition fit the descriptions of both Plutarch and ibn Ezra.

3 And Esther spoke again before the king, and fell down at his feet, and solicited him with tears to put away the mischief of Haman the Agagite, and his plan that he had contrived against the Jews.

4 Then the king held out to Esther the golden scepter. So Esther arose, and stood before the king.

5 And she said: 'If it please the king, and if I have found favor before him, and the thing seem right before the king, and I be pleasing in his eyes, let it be written to reverse the letters devised by Haman the son of Hammedatha the Agagite, which he wrote to destroy the Jews that are in all the king's provinces;

6 for how can I endure to see the evil that shall come to my people? and how can I endure to see the destruction of my kindred?'

7 Then the king Achashverosh said to Esther the queen and to Mordecai the Jew: 'Behold, I have given Esther the house of Haman, and him they have hanged upon the gallows, because he laid his hand on the Jews.

The king warns the people against carrying out Haman's decree. But that is in itself insufficient since a royal decree cannot be overturned -- even though the protagonist is no longer alive.

The language of the sentence states that Haman had already "laid his hand upon the Jews." עַל אֲשֶׁר-שָׁלַח יָדוֹ --That is, persecutions had already been carried out against Jews for several years, throughout the kingdom. Only the final decree had yet to be executed.

Mordecai had watched while his people suffered. He engaged Esther and insisted on her help only in response to the existential threat decreed by Haman in the king's hand. Esther, though alerted to the cause late in the game, now acts to reverse what would have been the "final solution."

8 Write concerning the Jews, as is good in your eyes, in the name of the king, and seal it with the king's ring; for the writing which is written in the king's name, and sealed with the king's ring, may no man reverse.'

One of the often ridiculed "facts" mentioned in both the first and 8th chapters of Esther as well as in the 6th chapter of Daniel is the inability of a Persian king to revoke one of his royally-issued decrees.

The first century BCE Greek historian Diodorus Siculus acknowledges this well-known law by describing the lament of Darius III in having to allow the execution of an innocent man for this very reason. Ibn Ezra sees this irrevocability as inviolable. This can be seen as a logical extrapolation of the king's quasi-divine infallible character, a gift from Ahura Mazda, the one God whose imprimatur accompanied every victorious relief uncovered in Persepolis, Susa or elsewhere.

9 Then were the king's scribes called at that time, in the third month, which is the month Sivan, on the twenty third day thereof; and it was written according to all that Mordecai commanded concerning the Jews, and to the satraps, and the governors and princes of the provinces which are from India unto Ethiopia, a hundred twenty and seven provinces, to every province according to the writing thereof, and to every people after their language, and to the Jews according to their writing, and according to their language.

This is Mordecai's first letter to the Jews throughout the kingdom. Later he is forced to send out another as is Esther, as will be seen below.

The kingdom did not actually comprise 127 provinces at this time. This is a reference to the inclusion of territory that did not come under Persian control until after Mordecai's ascension to power. The author, living sometime after these events, includes this reference a second time to remind the reader of the identity of the king, Achashverosh.

10 And they wrote in the name of king Achashverosh, and sealed it with the king's ring, and sent letters by messengers on horseback, riding on swift steeds that were used in the king's service, bred of the stud;

11 that the king had granted the Jews that were in every city to gather themselves together, and to stand for their life, to destroy, and to slay, and to cause to perish, all the forces of the people and province that would assault them, their little ones and women, and to take the spoil of them for a prey,

The Greek version of the *Book of Esther* was probably written shortly after the Maccabean rebellion. Its text actually ends with a brief identifier of the time and monarchy under which it was introduced (second century B.C.E. Egypt).

What is more, emendations to the Greek text include a description of a divine prophecy communicated to Mordecai in a dream, Esther's lengthy supplication to God on behalf of her people, and the king's entire letter authorizing the Jews to attack their tormentors in the name of "the Most High, the Most Mighty Living God. "

The language of this letter is the same as that of the original in describing the complete annihilation of the adversary. Only the taking of spoils will be resisted by the Jews

12 on one day in all the provinces of king Achashverosh, namely, on the thirteenth day of the twelfth month, which is the month Adar.

Later, in Chapter 9, verse13, Esther will ask for a second day to respond to attacks in Shushan, not out of vengefulness as some historians have suggested, but because the gentiles had the legal right to continue attacking the Jews while the Jews had the right to fight back only on the 13th of Adar. Esther asked for the 14th of Adar as well fearing a continued attack in the city where most of the Jews lived.

As a further discouragement to attacks, Esther requested that the sons of Haman be publically hanged (9:6-15).

13 The copy of the writing, to be given out as a legal decree in every province, was to be published to all the peoples, and that the Jews should be ready against that day to avenge themselves on their enemies.

14 So the messengers that rode on swift steeds that were used in the king's service went out, hurried and pressed on by the king's command; and the decree was given out in Shushan the castle.

The decree against the Jews was given out in the city itself, not the castle. On the other hand, here, the new decree would be heard by the royal host well before it would be heard by the people of the land. Esther wanted to be certain that the Jews had the overt support of all who occupied the palace and its immediate grounds. And from those grounds Mordecai went out as royalty so that the Jews of the city of Shushan could overcome what must have been a feeling of utter disbelief (verse 15 that follows).

15 And Mordecai went forth from the presence of the king in royal apparel of blue and white, and with a great crown of gold, and with a robe of fine linen and purple; and the city of Shushan shouted and was glad.

16 The Jews had light and gladness, and joy and honor.

17 And in every province, and in every city, wherever the king's commandment and his decree came, the Jews had gladness and joy, a feast and a holiday. And many from among the peoples of the land became Jews; for the fear of the Jews was fallen upon them.

The news of this sudden reversal of fortune was cause for a "yom tov," an actual holiday of celebration. Work was suspended and the Jews acknowledged the hand of divine providence that was so apparent.

Seeing this deliverance from certain doom along with the knowledge that the Jews would be taking up arms against their enemies, many gentiles chose to join the Jews. Whether for reasons of faith or fear, conversion to Judaism was a reaction not unheard of in the ancient world (the erev rav at the Exodus, for example).

Esther Chapter 9

1 And in the twelfth month, which is the month Adar, on its thirteenth day, when the king's commandment and his decree drew near to be carried out, in the day that the enemies of the Jews hoped to rule over them; it was turned to the contrary, the Jews instead ruled over those who hated them;

Why was this day chosen, both for the destruction of the Jews and subsequently as one of the days for the observance of the Purim holiday?

The holiday of Purim described in the *Book of Esther* had no overt religious character. Even after the defeat of Haman, the royal, pagan changes to Zoroastrianism were retained by the Persians. Jews would have to exist in an uncomfortable environment in which idol worship was pervasive. That made it all the more important that in ancient Persia the new Jewish holiday coincided with a Persian festival in which it could "hide" -- one which corresponded to the 5 days on which the Gemara (TB Megillah) states that the Megillah may be read. The Persian festival, called Farwardigan (the Persian new year festival whose name is related to the word Pur/lots), also included sending portions to one another and gifts to the poor (Hoschander).

There is some modern confusion about the names of the ancient Zoroastrian and Babylonian holidays. Farwardigan is known by some as a 5-day holiday of the dead. In fact, in modern Iran it is commemorated as a memorial day for the dead. One of the six annual Zoroastrian harvest holidays may also have coincided with Purim. The ancient Zoroastrian calendar included 365 days (12, thirty day months with five extra days added after the ninth month) with an adjustment once in 120 years (a leap year adding an additional 30-day month). But each of the major holidays was celebrated as a festival for 5 days. The Babylonian New Year, celebrated for 10, was absorbed into Zoroastrian practice as well.

Dieulafoy found in his archaeological excavations at Susa (Shushan) a quadrangular prism bearing different numbers on its four faces. This prism was likely a part of the observance of the Babylonian New Year festival known to some as Zagmuku. All of the gods of the Babylonians were "gathered" (so to speak) at that time for an audience with Marduk, the king of this heavenly menagerie. Marduk would "draw lots" to determine the fates for the year ahead. Since Haman drew lots on the first of Nissan (New Year's Day), his actions were in keeping with traditional practice for the evolving Zoroastrian polytheism.

2 the Jews gathered themselves together in their cities throughout all the provinces of the king Achashverosh, to lay hand on those who sought their hurt; and no man could withstand them; for the fear of them was fallen upon all the peoples.

3 And all the princes of the provinces, and the satraps, and the governors, and they that did the king's business, helped the Jews; because the fear of Mordecai was fallen upon them.

Mordecai had suddenly become an officer of such high standing that pleasing him became tantamount to pleasing the king.

4 For Mordecai was great in the king's house, and his fame went forth throughout all the provinces; for the man Mordecai waxed greater and greater.

5 And the Jews smote all their enemies with the stroke of the sword, and with slaughter and destruction, and did what they wanted with those who hated them.

6 And in Shushan the castle the Jews slew and destroyed five hundred men.

Where did the Jews kill five hundred men? They did so in Shushan HaBira, the palace, where they most likely had to engage soldiers and dignitaries. But in verse 15 below the text once again differentiates between Shushan HaBira and Shushan itself.

7 And Parshandatha, and Dalphon, and Aspatha,

8 and Poratha, and Adalia, and Aridatha,

9 and Parmashta, and Arisai, and Aridai, and Vaizatha,

10 the ten sons of Haman the son of Hammedatha, the Jews' enemy, slew they; but on the spoil they laid not their hand.

11 On that day the number of those that were slain in Shushan the castle was brought before the king.

12 And the king said unto Esther the queen: 'The Jews have slain and destroyed five hundred men in Shushan the castle, and the ten sons of Haman; what then have they done in the rest of the king's provinces! Now whatever thy petition, it shall be granted thee; and whatever thy request further, it shall be done.'

There is an indication of exasperation or shock on the part of the king in the language of this verse. He may be asking Esther, "If the Jews have already killed 500 in the palace, the destruction must have been much worse elsewhere in my kingdom. Is this not enough? Is there yet more that you will request?"

13 Then said Esther: 'If it please the king, let it be granted to the Jews that are in Shushan to do tomorrow also according unto this day's decree, and let Haman's ten sons be hanged upon the gallows.

Remember in chapter 8:12 the king grants the Jews one day to attack their tormentors. Here Esther uses her powers of persuasion to allow the Jews to continue attacking their foes while simultaneously holding before them the public image of Haman's sons on the gallows. The sons of Haman had already been killed, but now their bodies were displayed to strike fear in the would-be attackers.

14 And the king commanded it to be done; and a decree was publicized in Shushan; and they hanged Haman's ten sons.

15 And the Jews that were in Shushan gathered themselves together on the fourteenth day also of the month Adar, and slew three hundred men in Shushan; but on the spoil they laid not their hand.

Weren't 500 men just killed in Shushan in verse 6? But that was in Shushan HaBira, the palace. So these men must have been unprotected by the royal family and may have included merchants and others with routine royal discourse. An additional 300 were now killed in the city itself.

16 And the other Jews that were in the king's provinces gathered themselves, and stood for their lives, and had rest from their enemies, and slew of them that hated them seventy five thousand--but on the spoil they laid not their hand

Even though the king's decree encouraged the Jews to take the spoil of those whom they had defeated, they pointedly did not. This must be contrasted with the behavior of Haman and the gentile tormentors of the Jews, for whom the spoils of their attack were an intended reward.

17 on the thirteenth day of the month Adar, and on the fourteenth day of the same they rested, and made it a day of feasting and gladness.

18 But the Jews that were in Shushan assembled together on the thirteenth day thereof, and on the fourteenth thereof; and on the fifteenth day of the same they rested, and made it a day of feasting and gladness.

19 Therefore do the Jews of the villages, that dwell in the unwalled towns, make the fourteenth day of the month Adar a day of gladness and feasting, and a holiday, and of sending portions one to another.

20 And Mordecai wrote these things, and sent letters to all the Jews that were in all the provinces of the king Achashverosh, both near and far,

21 to enjoin them that they should keep the fourteenth day of the month Adar, and the fifteenth day of the same, yearly,

22 that the days that the Jews had rest from their enemies, and the month which was turned for them from sorrow to gladness,

and from mourning into a holiday; that they should make them days of feasting and gladness, and of sending portions one to another, and gifts to the poor.

Today, the holiday of Purim retains both the customs of sending portions to one another (to at least two others) and giving gifts to the poor (in the form of money with which they can buy food). In addition, two additional mitzvoth have been added: listening to a public reading of the *Book of Esther*, both in the evening and the following morning, and eating a festive meal.

23 And the Jews took upon themselves as they had begun to do, and as Mordecai had written to them;

24 because Haman the son of Hammedatha, the Agagite, the enemy of all the Jews, had plotted against the Jews to destroy them, and had cast pur, that is, the lot, to discomfit them, and to destroy them;

25 but when it came before the king, he commanded with letters that his wicked plan, which he had devised against the Jews, should be his own head; and that he and his sons should be hanged on the gallows.

26 Therefore they called these days Purim, after the name of pur. Therefore because of all the words of this letter, and of that which they had seen concerning this matter, and that which had happened to them,

27 the Jews ordained, and accepted upon them, and upon their seed, and upon all such as joined themselves to them, so as it should not fail, that they would keep these two days according to its writing and according to its appointed time every year;

Mordecai and Esther surely realized that by establishing Purim in those days of the month of Adar, it would disguise a lack of participation by the Jews in the pagan festival (a Babylonian festival added to Zoroastrian worship during the reign of Artaxerxes II).

Most of the Jews accepted Mordecai's decree in the first letter, but the more religious Jews may have feared that the rank and file would ultimately confuse the Jewish and pagan celebrations, forgetting the significance of the day. They may have actively campaigned against the decree of Mordecai thereby necessitating Esther's second letter.

Purim was observed as a largely secular festival – the only biblical festival on which work is permitted. "Originally, in accordance with Esther 9:19, Purim was intended as a yom tov in which no work would be done, but later in Mordecai's letter of Purim, it was established only as days of feasting and gladness, but not as yom tov." (Talmud Bavli, Megillah 5b) Ultimately the religious leaders capitulated and later added the public reading of the Megillah to consolidate the Jewish nature of the day.

28 and that these days should be remembered and kept throughout every generation, every family, every province, and every city; and that these days of Purim should not pass from among the Jews, nor the memory of them perish from their seed.

The author of the *Book of Esther* is describing these events a generation or two after they took place. If the events took place during the rule of Artaxerxes II then a start had been made on rebuilding the Temple in Jerusalem only to be halted by this monarch.

The writer is a Persian Jew familiar with the entirety of Mordecai's political career -- and living after his passing but before the conquest of Persia by Alexander the Great and the Greeks. He knows that the observance of the holiday is as he describes and has been since its inception.

29 Then Esther the queen, the daughter of Avichail, and Mordecai the Jew, wrote down all the acts of power, to confirm this second letter of Purim.

Why was this second letter of Mordecai and Esther needed when the festival of Purim had already been established and accepted? This is a further indication that there was resistance among the more traditionally religious Jews.

They had convinced many of their co-religionists to reject the observance of the "secular" holiday as described in Mordecai's first letter. Only in verse 32 is it stated that "the commandment of Esther confirmed these matters of Purim." Secular Jews would only have objected if pressured by their religious leaders since observance of the holiday implied no religious burden, coincided with a major secular holiday and was simply celebratory in nature.

30 And he sent letters to all the Jews, to the one hundred and twenty seven provinces of the kingdom of Achashverosh, with words of peace and truth,

31 to confirm these days of Purim in their appointed times, as Mordecai the Jew and Esther the queen had enjoined them, and as they had ordained for themselves and for their seed, the matters of the fastings and their cry.

32 And the commandment of Esther confirmed these matters of Purim; and it was written in the book.

The book in question would be the royal chronicles, subsequently destroyed in the Alexandrian conquest.

Esther Chapter 10

1 And the king Achashverosh laid a tribute upon the land, and upon the isles of the sea.

2 And all the acts of his power and of his might, and the full account of the greatness of Mordecai, how the king advanced

him, are they not written in the book of the chronicles of the kings of Media and Persia?

3 For Mordecai the Jew was second to king Achashverosh, and great among the Jews, and accepted by the multitude/majority of his brethren; seeking the good of his people and speaking peace to all his seed.

Like Joseph, Mordecai rose to sudden prominence and helped lead a gentile monarch to greatness. Yet the language of this verse can mean that he was only accepted by the "majority" of his fellow Jews. Subsequent objections to the holiday itself involve disputes among the sages of the Talmud as well as local leaders and Biblical commentators.

"God knits human deeds and their issues with His wise design – the ennui of the sleepless night of a king; the fleeting emotion of a moment in a kingly breast – and behold, averted is the blow from the helpless, from those whose only possession is God! The finely calculated flash of lightning laden with destruction is hurled back upon the head of him who released it, and Israel, defenseless Israel, summoned itself to defend its life, emerges from the danger which threatened it with darkness and destruction – emerges into light and gladness." (*Horeb*, Samson Rafael Hirsch, Section 247a)

Additional Reference Bibliography

Boyce, Mary; **Zoroastrians: Their Religious Beliefs and Practices**, 2007, Routledge, London.

Bury, John Bagnell; **The Ancient Greek Historians**, 2011, Ulan Press.

Curtis and Tallis; **Forgotten Empire: The World of Ancient Persia**, 2005, British Museum Press, London.

Goodspeed, Edgar J.: **The Apocrypha**, 1989, Vintage Books, New York.

Hartman, David; **A Living Covenant**, 1997, Jewish Lights, Woodstock, VT.

Hirsch, Samson Raphael; **Horeb**, 1962, Soncino Press, London.

Hoschander, Jacob; **The Book of Esther in the Light of History**, 1923, The Dropsie College, Philadelphia, PA.

Johnson, Ken; **Ancient Seder Olam**, 1997, Xulon Press.

Lincoln, Bruce: **Religion, Empire and Torture: The Case of Achaemenian Persia with a Postscript of Abu Ghraib**, 2007, University of Chicago Press.

Porten, Bezalel; **Archives from Elephantine**: The Life of an Ancient Jewish Military Colony, 1968. University of California Press, Berkeley, CA.

Schiffman, Lawrence H.; **Reclaiming the Dead Sea Scrolls**, 1994, Jewish Publication Society, Philadelphia, PA.

Urbach, Epjraim E.; **The Sages**, 1975 Harvard University Press, Cambridge, MA.

Vermes, Geza; **The Story of the Scrolls**, 2010, Penguin Books, New York.

Walfish, Barry, **Jewish Quarterly Review**, *The Two Commentaries of Abraham ibn Ezra on the Book of Esther*, April, 1989, p. 323-343.

Whiston, William; **The Works of Josephus**, 1987, Hendrickson Publishers, Peabody, MA.

Zaehner, Robert Charles: **The Dawn and Twilight of Zoroastrianism**, 1961, Phoenix Press, London.